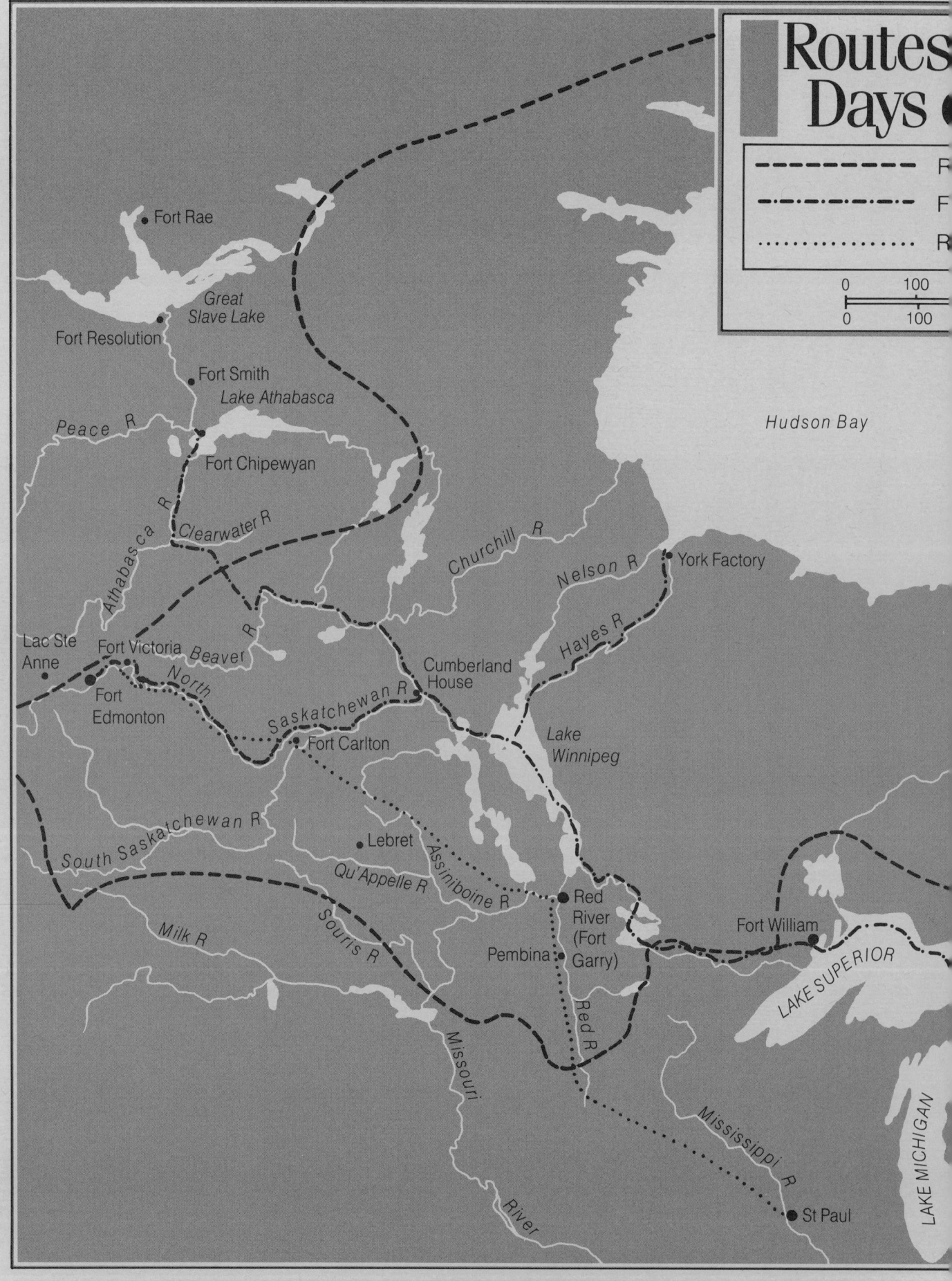

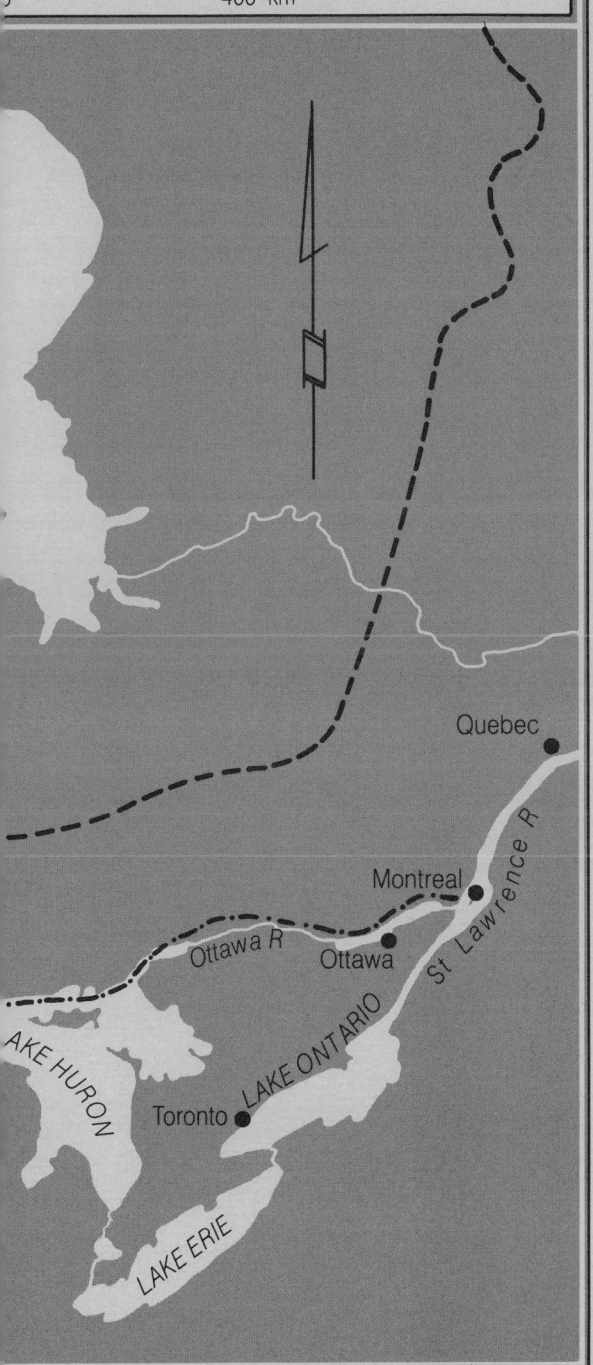

Portrait of a Metis man. Courtesy St. Boniface Historical Society

METIS

	DATE DUE		
MAR 1 8 2005			

METIS
People between Two Worlds

Julia D. Harrison

The Glenbow-Alberta Institute
in association with
Douglas & McIntyre
Vancouver/Toronto

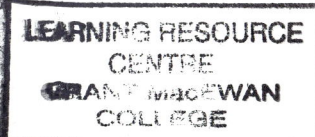

Copyright © 1985 by Glenbow-Alberta Institute

All rights reserved. No part of this book may be reproduced or transmitted in any form by any means without permission in writing from the publisher, except by a reviewer, who may quote brief passages in a review.

Douglas & McIntyre Ltd.
1615 Venables Street
Vancouver, B. C.
V5L 2H1

Canadian Cataloguing in Publication Data

Harrison, Julia D. (Julia Diane), 1953–
    Metis, people between two worlds

Includes index.
Bibliography: p.
ISBN 0-88894-421-7

1. Métis — History.*   I. Title.
FC109.H37 1985   971'.00497   C85-091013-7
E99.M693H37 1985

Book design by Barbara Hodgson
Typesetting by Evergreen Press Ltd.
Printed and bound in Canada by D. W. Friesen & Sons Ltd.

Contents

	Acknowledgements	7
INTRODUCTION	The Metis People	8
CHAPTER ONE	A Free and Independent People: To 1885	16
	An Expressive Individuality: Personal and Household Items	48
CHAPTER TWO	Change and the Struggle to Survive: 1885 to 1920	54
	An Independent Style: Early Metis Clothing	84
CHAPTER THREE	Poverty and a Passion for Politics: 1920 to 1949	90
CHAPTER FOUR	Rekindling the Fires: 1950 to 1969	120
CHAPTER FIVE	Towards Recognition and Justice: 1970 to 1985	136
	Notes	151
	Bibliography	155
	Index	158

*To the Forgotten People,
who will be remembered*

Acknowledgements

Working on this book and the Glenbow Museum exhibition related to it has been a great privilege for me. I owe thanks to many people for the opportunity to do both, and for the support and encouragement that I received along the way. To the many Metis people who helped me and taught me such a great deal, I owe a large debt of gratitude.

To Gulf Canada Limited and the National Museums of Canada, which provided generous support for the exhibition, and to the Province of Alberta and the City of Calgary for their continuing support of Glenbow, I wish to express my sincere appreciation.

Ted Brasser of the National Museum of Man was most generous in giving me access to his entire research files, which proved to be a valuable resource. Many of my museum colleagues in institutions across the country deserve special mention for their assistance and generosity, particularly Judy Hall and Judy Thompson of the National Museum of Man.

To Dr. Hugh Dempsey, Chief Curator at the Glenbow Museum, who implanted the idea for the project in my mind several years ago and then let me develop it on my own, offering valuable advice, assistance and friendship when needed, I am deeply grateful. Ms. Lindsay Moir, Reference Librarian at the Glenbow, facilitated my research greatly by her diligent pursuit of print material. The staff of my department at times were left for long periods to work on their own but always supported me totally: Kathy Zedde and Dennis Slater, research assistants for the project; Laurie Jessenberger, who provided clerical help, and Anne Williams, who typed the almost unreadable preliminary drafts of the manuscript but who always assured me that "whatever it takes, it will be done." My debt to them is very great.

My friends and family helped me through the many weary moments, and I thank them for their insightful comments on the manuscript.

It was a privilege and an honour to work with Ruth Fraser as my editor, but most importantly, it was a great pleasure.

Please note that, unless indicated otherwise, the term "Metis" is used throughout this book to refer to all those of Native and European ancestry. Furthermore, the spelling of Metis without an accent is that used by contemporary Metis associations.

All opinions expressed are my own, and I accept responsibility for all errors.

Julia D. Harrison
Curator, Ethnology Department
Glenbow Museum

Introduction

The Metis People

When Louis Riel died on the gallows in 1885, it was said that the Metis nation died with him; yet, a century later in the Constitution, the Canadian government recognized the Metis as one of the aboriginal peoples of Canada. Either the Metis have been resurrected from the dead (as Riel predicted he would be), or they never did die, this "new nation" born of the Native and European peoples of Canada.

In the seventeenth century furs were in great demand in Europe, and the search for this valuable commodity brought an influx of adventurers and entrepreneurs to the northern shores of North America. Some historians claim that the first Metis was born nine months after these Europeans arrived. Primarily engaged in the fur trade, the men quickly sought the companionship and support of Indian women, for the various Native peoples who trapped the coveted furs were not always friendly, and the wilderness environment was often hostile. These Indian women ensured the survival of the European men by supplying them with appropriate clothing such as moccasins, snowshoes and buckskin jackets, food from the wild, and family ties to Native groups and trading partners.

The new population of mixed Native and white ancestry stemmed not only from the French who settled along the St. Lawrence River, but also from the English and Scottish fur traders who later established contact with Native groups in the area around Hudson Bay. Initially, the mixed-blood people were not distinguished in any way, being classed according to their ancestry and lifestyle as English (which included Scottish), French or Native. Only later did they become known as Metis.

The word "Metis" comes from the Latin *miscere*, meaning "to mix," and was used originally to describe the children of Native mothers and French fathers. Another term for the Metis is derived from the Ojibwa word *wissakodewinmi*, which means "half-burnt woodmen," describing their lighter complexion in comparison to that of full-blooded Indians. The French picked up the translation and often used the term *bois brûlé*, or "burnt-wood," for these people. They were also called by various other names, including Country-born, Black Scots, Métis anglaise, Breeds and Half-breeds. The term "Half-breed" generally became the most frequently used, though in the mid-twentieth century it became unpopular among some

Pages 8/9: *A Half-breed hunters' camp, 1874. Courtesy Public Archives of Canada, C-81767*

A Halfcast and His Two Wives, *a watercolour by Peter Rindisbacher, 1825 or 1826. The items of clothing that they are wearing are typical of early descriptions. Courtesy M. Knoedler & Co. Inc., 20329*

mixed-blood people who adamantly insisted "we're not helf [*sic*] men, we're full men." Others, however, regarded it as an acceptable word.

In this book the terms "Metis" and "Half-breed" are used interchangeably for all people with mixed Native and white ancestry.

In western Canada the mixed-blood population was not a homogeneous group. The European part of their heritage could have been French, English, Scottish, Irish or Scandinavian, though most of their Native ancestors were Cree or Ojibwa. The nature of the fur trade demanded that traders travel great distances across the North American continent, so their wives often came from a variety of groups.

Popular attitudes ascribe stereotyped characteristics to various European nationalities: the French fun-loving, the English reserved and the Scottish dour. Native groups allegedly had similar traits, which they passed on to their descendants. Parallel broad generalizations were made about the French Metis, who were described by two observers, Milton and Cheadle, as "a merry, light-hearted, obliging race, recklessly generous, hospitable, and extravagant. . . . Completely under the influence of the priests . . . and observing the outward forms of their religion with great regularity, they are grossly immoral, often dishonest and generally not trustworthy. . . . But as hunters, guides and voyageurs, they are unequalled." English Half-breeds, on the other hand, were said to prefer the "pursuit of husbandry to the chase, and [to] follow close on the heels of the Scotch in the path of industry and moral rectitude." These and other generalizations, however, represent the views and biases of Europeans, whose standards differed from those of the Metis.

One consistent characteristic that describes the Metis is implicit in the name the Cree gave to them, *o-tee-paym-soo-wuk*, which means "their own boss." Never a group to be herded, channelled or manipulated, the Metis have constantly reaffirmed their independence. As one Metis writer said, "Unlike many other minority groups, the Metis are basically non-conformist."

Right from the beginning the Metis could not be classified by a definitive set of criteria. Their language was described by one visitor to a Metis camp as "polyglot jabber" and by another as "*toute mêlé*," or "all mixed." It may well have included "a fine broad Scotch, a scattering of Gaelic and Irish brogue and a plentiful mixture of rapidly uttered French patois that would drive a Parisian mad," as well as elements of native languages. For instance, the language spoken by Metis in the Turtle Mountain area of South Dakota, called *michif*, is essentially a dialect of Cree with a smattering of several other languages.

By the nineteenth century the Metis of western Canada fell into three broad groups: those who worked in the fur trade as post factors, clerks, interpreters, canoemen and packers; those who led semisettled lives on small farms or plots where they grew grain and raised livestock; and finally, those who were hunters and trappers. Some worked in all areas of employ during their careers, depending on the resources available. Whatever their occupation and whether they lived in the "civilized" setting of

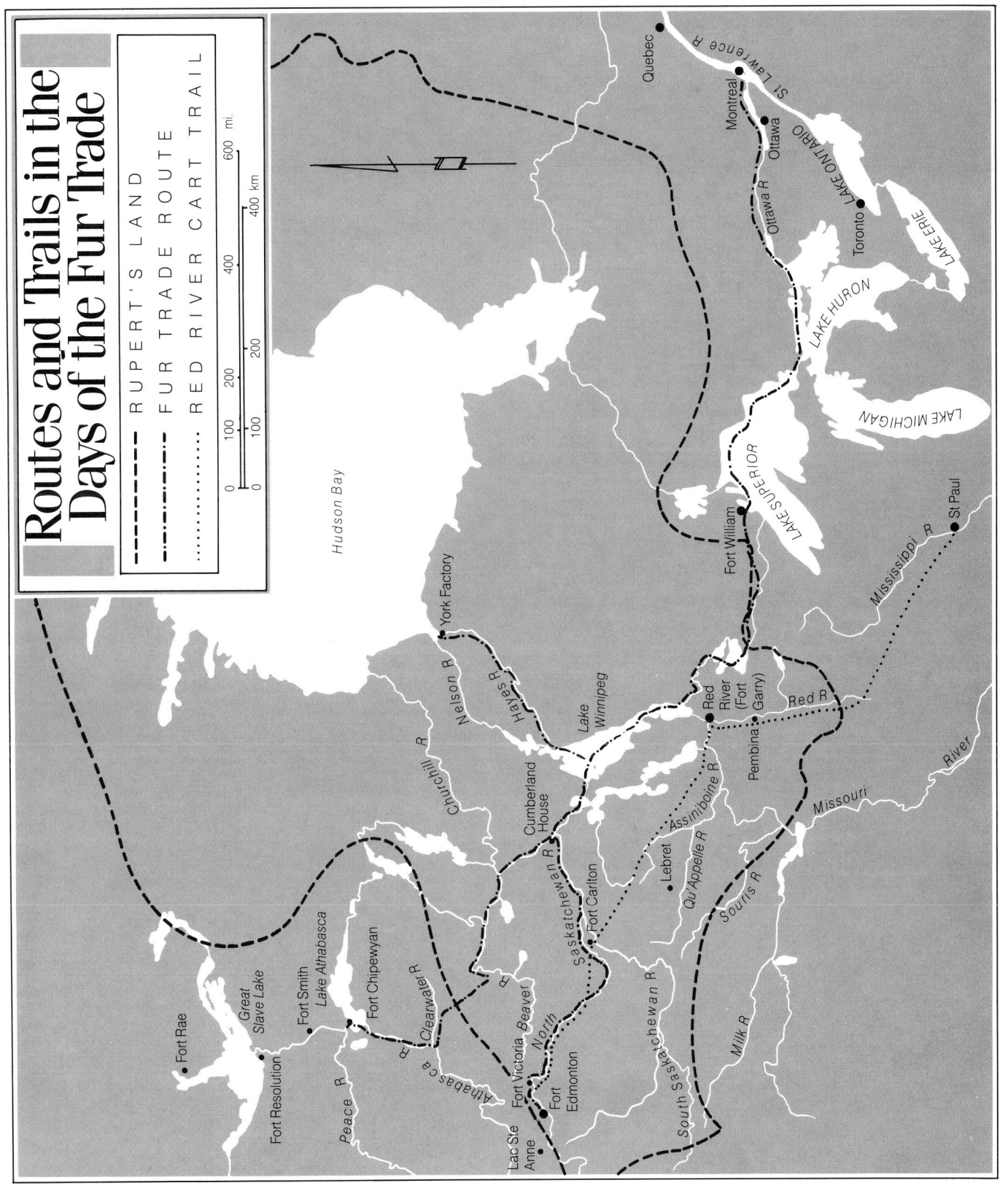

Red River or out along the many traplines in the hinterland, the Metis were part of a continuum having Native roots at one end and European at the other.

As a result of their mixed heritage, it is "easier to define what is *not* a signal for Metis than isolating one that is." This may explain why items of Metis origin have been neglected in "Canada's galleries, museums, art centres and other cultural institutions." Metis beadwork and craftwork has often been classed as Indian, and their handmade furniture has usually been attributed to pioneers. Thus, much of what the Metis produced has been buried in museum collections under other names or ignored altogether.

Because the Metis of western Canada played a major role in the fur trade, they had a sense of national consciousness that was strengthened by their concentration in the Red River area. This led them to declare themselves, in the early nineteenth century, a "new nation."

In recent years, the Metis National Council, which represents the mixed-blood population of western Canada, has been insisting that the word "Metis" refers only to those who can trace their roots to the intermixing of whites and Natives in western Canada. In the council's view, peoples of mixed ancestry in other areas are Nonstatus Indians, and only the Metis of western Canada have a sense of being one "nation" with its own identity.

Nonstatus Indians are a somewhat confusing group; the term most often refers to those men, their families and their descendants who did not take treaty or were forced out, or to women who married white men (and the children of these marriages) or Metis.

Because both Metis and Nonstatus Indians are peoples of Native ancestry striving to improve their economic, social and political standing, they are often thought of as being the same; but the most viable solutions to their problems are often quite different, and each group should be considered separately.

Although the Metis have a mixed ancestry, they see themselves as different and separate from both Indians and whites. Throughout history, relations between the Metis and their two ancestral groups have been openly hostile at times: they clashed with white Canadians in 1869–70 and again in 1885. The relationship between the Metis and the Indians has often been stormy, as Maria Campbell noted in her book, *Halfbreed:* "There never was much love lost between Indians and Halfbreeds. They were completely different from us — quiet when we were noisy . . . Indians were very passive . . . whereas Halfbreeds were quick-tempered — quick to fight, but quick to forgive and forget." In many largely native communities, the current relationships between Indians and Metis vary from supportive and often affectionate to hostile and antagonistic.

Who, then, are the Metis of the twentieth century? A glimpse of the roots of the Metis people in the early years of the fur trade indicates that even though they had a common historical background, they were not a cohesive group possessing one culture and language. Today it is difficult to identify the Metis as a unified group apart from the rest of the Canadian population. They no longer have separate languages, wear distinctive styles of dress or have definite physical similarities. Nor do they all live in the same region or follow the same line of work. Many have joined the larger society. A list of those Canadians with at least one Native ancestor in their family tree would (by one estimate) include forty per cent of the French-Canadian population, and in English-speaking Canada would include individuals as diverse as the late Norman Bethune, the famous Canadian doctor, hockey player Brian Trottier and Premier Peter Lougheed of Alberta. (Current figures for the Metis are difficult to determine: the 1981 census counted 98 200 Metis, but various Metis associations claim that there are many more, depending on the criteria used.)

According to a twentieth-century leader of the Metis, Stan Daniels, the Metis have found themselves "caught in the vacuum of two cultures with neither fully accepting [them]." The marginality of the Metis — who have not been given either the resources and rights of Indians or full access to white society and its advantages — has created an almost negative identity: "they are Metis because they are not somebody else."

But many contemporary Metis have a clear sense of their own identity as they individually define it; and in Canada, a country constantly seeking to establish a sense of identity, the Metis see themselves as a distinctive people. In their 1979 Declaration of Metis Rights, they stated that they were "the true spirit of Canada and are the source of Canadian identity."

Chapter One

A Free & Independent People To 1885

Born as the result of unions between Native women and European fur traders, the mixed-blood people of Canada were sometimes called "the children of the fur trade." The fur trade, which had begun on the east coast in the sixteenth century, had quickly spread inland west to the prairies and had come under the control of two major trading companies: the Hudson's Bay Company, chartered in 1670, with headquarters in England, and the North West Company, which had its beginnings in 1779, based in Montreal. By 1800 a fierce rivalry was entrenched between the two firms over the fur trade in the vast North-West, then populated sparsely by the Native people whose land it was, a couple of hundred white traders living in forts and a growing number of Metis. Although many of the traders eventually returned home to Montreal or Europe, the Metis, like their Indian relatives, knew no other home but the North-West, and many of them worked for the two trading companies as guides, canoemen, traders, hunters and trappers, as well as in just about every other aspect of the fur trade.

Stemming from their heritage of the French-Canadian voyageurs who travelled the arduous and hazardous route from Montreal to various points in the

West, the French Metis possessed an intense sense of joie de vivre, while from their Native heritage they had a knowledge of survival in the wilderness. Proud of their strength, endurance, daring and skills, the voyageurs developed a strong esprit de corps as well as a distinctive style of dress for which they became known. A blue capote, a beaded pipe bag that hung from a bright red sash and the inevitable pipe became standard items for many of them. These men readily worked sixteen to eighteen hours a day, paddling the precious loads of trade goods through fast-flowing waterways and turbulent rapids or hauling the canoes and three tons (2.7 t) of freight over long, arduous portages. Their day began at two A.M., with a six-hour paddle until breakfast. Lunch at midday consisted of pemmican eaten in the canoe, with no stop made until well after dusk, when camp was made and supper was served. Once every hour, however, paddling ceased and each man lit his pipe; because they stopped for a smoke every four or five miles (6 or 8 km), the routes were measured in "pipes." Today the descendants of the tripmen, many of whom are trappers in the northern regions of Canada, still measure their traplines in "pipes."

On some routes, large, sturdy York boats replaced birchbark canoes, and many Metis tripmen became skilled oarsmen as they travelled on Lake Winnipeg or along the Saskatchewan River. These York boats had been introduced by Hudson's Bay Company employees who had come from the Orkney Islands of northern Scotland. They married Native women and taught their Half-breed children how to build the York boats, which resembled the fishing boats of the Orkneys. These large boats were up to forty-two feet (12.6 m) long and were capable of carrying six tons (5.4 t) of cargo. A crew of at least ten men was needed to manoeuvre them, as often the heavy vessels had to be dragged through rough rapids and over portages on a bed of rollers or cut logs, testing the strength and skill of the toughest men.

Not all the Metis were voyageurs or tripmen. Both the Hudson's Bay Company and the North West Company hired some men as clerks and post managers, particularly those who had been educated in the east or in Britain. The fact that their fathers had sent them away for schooling is proof that they were committed to their mixed-blood children. Some worked as interpreters in the forts or became servants and tradesmen. Many, particularly those who lived close to their Native relatives, were trappers, and some were fishermen, supplying the forts with food in the winter months. Most significantly, however, many Metis were buffalo hunters and suppliers of pemmican, which was made from dried buffalo meat and was a staple food for the entire fur trade.

Family bonds among the Metis were very strong. This was rooted in the traditions of their Native ancestors and those of the early traders who chose to leave behind their former lives and remain in this country with their new families. To many of these Europeans, their wives had become far more than a convenience.

Whatever tasks these people pursued, there was a genuine bonding and camaraderie between them and a strong desire to protect their adventurous and

Pages 16/17: A troupe of weary freighters stop for a pipe along one of the cart trails out of Red River, circa 1858. Note the variety of their clothing. Photograph by B. F. Upton, courtesy Minnesota Historical Society, 405

profitable but rugged lifestyle. Their freedom was threatened in 1811, when Lord Selkirk founded the Red River colony. An agriculturally based community had never been considered viable in the West, and the North West Company was violently opposed to the idea because the settlement would lie directly on its main trade route from Montreal through the Great Lakes, along the Red River and out to the western regions and north to the Athabasca River.

In an attempt to heighten antagonism towards the Red River settlement, the North West Company fuelled the idea of a territory and nation that had begun to develop among the Metis. The company warned them that the influx of settlers into the territory would spell the end of their lifestyle, freedom and individuality. Fearing this to be true, the people appointed Cuthbert Grant as "Captain General of all half-breeds in the country" in 1816. Under his leadership, the French and English Half-breeds began to assert their claim to an aboriginal title to the country and demand compensation from the white settlers."

That same year, Governor Semple of the Red River colony had cut off the pemmican supply routes of the North West Company. Grant planned to re-open those routes and set out with a large party of Metis towards the colony; they were met en route by Governor Semple and a group of settlers. A shot was fired, and in the exchange of gunfire that followed, Semple and twenty-one of his men were killed. Grant lost one man in the skirmish, which became known as the Battle of Seven Oaks. The Metis felt that they had firmly established themselves as a force to be considered in any future developments in the area.

Decades of intense rivalry between the North West Company and the Hudson's Bay Company resulted in overtrapping; in addition, the whimsical dictates of fashion in Europe caused the popularity of the beaver felt hat to fade and be replaced with the dashing silk top hat. These events had an adverse effect on the fur trade, and the two companies found themselves in financial trouble. Retaining the name of the Hudson's Bay Company, they merged in 1821, creating serious changes in the lives of the mixed-blood people who worked for them. Each company had often built forts in proximity to those of the other company in an effort to take control of certain areas. When the two companies merged, many of the forts became redundant and were abandoned, leaving a number of mixed-blood employees without a means of support. These families were encouraged to move to the Red River area and adopt a more stable way of life based on agriculture. Many Metis willingly moved there as they could increase their participation in the pemmican trade. Although some Metis did become farmers, others chose to remain hunters, trappers and fishermen in small settlements, where their way of life was closely related to that of their Native ancestors.

The Hudson's Bay Company encouraged the development of Christian missions in Red River to "raise the moral standards of the people and ensure a greater degree of social stability." In turn, the missionaries fostered the idea of agricultural settlement among the Metis, who had been leading mobile and independent lives. In order to have continuing influence over the Metis, the priests knew that more permanent settlements were necessary.

The first Roman Catholic missionaries arrived in 1818, creating a force that was to aid in establishing a sense of nationhood — through the bonds of Catholicism — in the hearts and minds of the mixed-blood people. The Reverend J. West was the first Anglican missionary to arrive in the colony in 1820. Several years later four members of the Catholic Order of the Grey Sisters of Charity and priests from the order of the Oblates of Mary Immaculate arrived from Quebec to assist the far-flung Native missions. The nuns and the Oblates were to work with the Metis and Native people for many years and had a significant influence on their future. In 1851 the first Presbyterian minister arrived in Red River to tend to the Scottish settlers.

Many of the French Metis were ardent Roman Catholics, the English Half-breeds staunch Anglicans and the Scottish mixed-bloods strict Presbyterian, while in areas such as Norway House, most were Methodist. Added to these Christian beliefs would have been elements of their maternal ancestors' Native religions, which some Metis continued to practise to the exclusion of Christianity.

The majority of residents in the Red River settlement were of mixed ancestry. The descendants of the English and Scottish Half-breeds seemed to be more willing to adapt to agriculture or business, and they formed one of the more stable groups in Red River, with ties based on kinship, a common social background and their Protestant faith.

Most of the French Metis also developed a strong bond of unity based largely on their Catholic faith and mobile lifestyle. The great buffalo hunts, which were held twice a year, became a focus of life in the Red River, particularly for the French Metis. The purpose of the spring hunt was to obtain a large supply of dried buffalo meat from which pemmican was made and traded to the Hudson's Bay Company to provision tripmen and traders who still sought furs in the hinterland. The smaller winter hunt was undertaken mainly to obtain meat and hides to see the Metis population through the winter, but also partly to supply food for the colony in poor crop years. For the government officials and church leaders who wished to see the Metis become stable farmers, the annual buffalo hunts were extremely disconcerting. But to the Metis the hunts provided a viable business venture as well as a food supply for themselves and often the colonists in Red River. Because the Red River area was repeatedly plagued with crop failures in those early years, the Metis had little incentive to become large-scale farmers and give up the independence, profit and challenge of the hunt.

Records for 1820 show that 540 carts left the settlement for Pembina in Minnesota, where the hunt actually began. By 1840 the numbers had increased to 1210 carts and 1630 people. There was an infectious enthusiasm around the hunt and its organization, with a great flurry of activity as entire families made all the preparations for the two-month adventure. At the encouragement of the French Metis who were devout Catholics and who dominated the hunt, and also in the interests of the Catholic church, a priest often went along on the hunt.

An integral part of the hunt was the famous Red River cart, so closely associated with the Metis that the Plains Indians had a special way of designating them in sign language. The fingers of each hand circled each other to represent cart wheels, and then a finger was drawn down to form half of the human body. Literally translated, the sign said a Metis was "half-wagon, half-man." The cart came from the European heritage of the Metis. Some sources trace it to carts used in Quebec in the early days of settlement there; others go directly back to Scotland. The carts were readily made from wood and could be drawn by either horses or oxen. The main frame was constructed of two large poles about twelve feet (3.6 m) in length, half forming the shafts to which the horse or oxen were harnessed, and the other half providing support for the frame, crowned with an "inelegent [sic] box." Five feet (1.5 m) in diameter, the wheels were made of several pieces of oak, wrapped with strips of buffalo hide called *shaganappi* to hold the segments together. The axle, usually made of oak, was "lashed to the cart with dampened strips of buffalo hide, which shrank as they dried," creating a firm grip.

The axles were probably the most famous part of the cart because the noise they made as the wheels turned was excruciating, and when several carts were travelling together, they could be heard within a three-mile (5-km) radius. Not wanting to grease the axles, which would then clog up with dust and mud, the cart drivers left them ungreased most of the time. One writer said that "Each cart [had] its own musical quality . . . one . . . has a deep bass voice and another is a fine tenor. One resembles a cathedral organ, another is like a fiddle, and another has the tinkling sound of a pair of brass cymbals." However, others complained that the noise made by the carts was "hellish" or made "your blood run cold" or compared it to "the scraping of a thousand finger nails on a thousand panes of glass."

Despite the fact that Red River carts were rather ramshackle affairs, each with "its own individual waggle," they met all conditions of travel. They could be "drawn through bogs," buoyed through river fords, and were "strong on rock strewn hills and hard to upset in stumpy forests." In winter the wheels were removed, and the frame was hitched to a horse to be pulled like a sleigh. A cart could even be made into a temporary boat by removing the wheels, strapping them to the bottom of the box and floating it on the river.

In the tradition of decorating household and personal items, Metis women often adorned their carts. As one editor of a local newspaper observed, "The carts of the women are painted; and have a cover with other appearances of greater attention to comfort than is displayed in the carts appropriated to the men."

The versatile Red River cart was used on the buffalo hunt to transport families and supplies, and with hundreds of them travelling together, they made a noisy, colourful parade. Once the throng made camp, the organization and structuring of the hunt itself began. Ten captains of the hunt were selected, with one senior captain who had authority over everything and everyone.

Strict rules of the camp were laid down by the group and enforced by the captains. These rules stated:

1. No buffalo to be run on the Sabbath-day.
2. No party to fork off, lag behind, or go before, without permission.
3. No person or party to run buffalo before the general order.
4. Every captain with his men, in turn, to patrol the camp, and keep guard.
5. For the first trespass against these laws, the offender to have his saddle and bridle cut up.
6. For the second offence, the coat to be taken off the offender's back, and be cut up.
7. For the third offence, the offender to be flogged.
8. Any person convicted of theft, even to the value of a sinew, to be brought to the middle of the camp, and the crier to call out his or her name three times, adding the word "Thief", at each time.

When camp was set up for the night, the men and officials would hold an evening council to discuss the events of that day and the line of march for the next. Each man would bring to the council his gun, his smoking bag and his pipe.

In addition to the horses that drew the carts, each hunter had his buffalo horse with him. Known as "runners," these

Half Breeds Running Buffalo, *a painting by Paul Kane, 1840s. The pad saddles, made by Metis, were commonly used by hunters. Courtesy Royal Ontario Museum, 912.1.26*

Left: A Metis family in a Red River cart, in a sketch by W. A. Rogers, published in Harper's Monthly, *1879. Courtesy Glenbow Museum, NA 1406-5*

Right: "Young" McKay, a Metis guide of a Red River cart train en route from Red River to St. Paul, in an engraving published in Harper's Monthly, *1860. Courtesy Glenbow Museum, NA 1406-10*

prized horses were used only for the hunt and at times for racing. They were "tended with all the care which the cavalier of old bestowed on his warsteed; ... [the] trappings were garnished with beads and porcupine quills, exhibiting all the skill which the hunter's wife or belle [could] exercise; while the head and tail display all the colours of the rainbow in the variety of ribbon attached to them." A Metis buffalo hunter took great pride in his horse; its speed and dependability were of utmost importance when he launched himself into a herd of huge, stampeding buffalo. Selecting one animal for the kill, the hunter took aim, often dispatching it with one shot. He then threw down a marker, such as a cap or a glove, beside his kill. While still mounted on his galloping horse, he poured gunpowder down the barrel of his rifle, reloaded it with shot and proceeded to slay another animal in the charging herd. A good horse and rider could be expected to kill as many as twelve buffalo in one day.

Following the kill, the women began the task of skinning and butchering the carcasses, saving the choice pieces but slicing the bulk of the meat into thin strips for pemmican. After these strips were sun dried thoroughly on racks, the women pounded the meat to shreds,

Top: Women cooking outdoors at a Metis camp near Pembina, in an engraving published in Harper's Weekly, 1859. Their dresses reflect the European heritage of the Metis. Courtesy Glenbow Museum, NA 1406-27

Bottom: A Metis buffalo hunters' camp at night, with Red River carts drawn up in a circle, in an engraving published in Harper's Monthly, 1879. Courtesy Glenbow Museum, NA 1406-4

A lively Metis dance at Pembina, in an engraving published in Harper's Monthly, *1860. Courtesy Glenbow Museum, NA 1406-23*

mixed it with buffalo tallow and berries, then poured it into buffalo-hide bags, making ninety-pound (40.5-kg) packs. Four pounds (1.8 kg) of meat yielded one pound (0.45 kg) of pemmican, a nourishing and very filling food that kept well.

During the Red River days, the hunt formed a major part of the social and economic fabric of the colony. When the spring hunt was over and the entire expedition had returned, the pemmican was sold to fur traders or given to the Hudson's Bay Company as payment for provisions that had been supplied on credit. Most of the hunters and their families went back to their river-lot homes on the Red River, and others returned to their traplines or outlying settlements.

A festive air accompanied the hunters back to the colony. Perhaps a large party would be held, as the spirit to dance was firmly ingrained in the Metis from their Native, Scottish and French ancestry. Their most famous dance, called the "Red River jig," included elements of Native dancing as well as the jigs and reels of the French and Scots.

Dances were energetic, with each couple, particularly the men, trying to outdo their companions. Many would dance until they had completely worn out a pair of moccasins. One affair at Norway House was described as including "polkas, galops, waltzes, *quadrilles, cotillions,* country dances, reels and jigs [and] employed the heels and talents of the assembly. There were cards for the infirm and lazy, brandy and tobacco for the thirsty and unremitting hospitality to all." The music was provided by a fiddle and "a brilliant accompaniment upon a large tin pan," as well as the clack of spoons.

Many Metis played the fiddle, an instrument inherited from both their Scottish and French ancestors. They were often handmade from maple wood and birch, as most Metis did not have the money to buy them ready-made. Although many were not formally trained in music, they were said to tune their fiddles to the "cry of the loon and the bellow of a rutting moose."

The Metis did not live quietly and sedately. If their regular dances were uproarious events, their daily lives were only slightly calmer. On Sundays, when most of them observed the Lord's Day by attending either a Roman Catholic mass or a Protestant service, the community had "all the appearance of a fair, and whether arriving or returning, the congregation [was] deafened by the clamour." Alexander Ross, a prominent member of the Red River colony, wrote that on any day the Metis were "passionately fond of roving about, visiting, card-playing, and making up gossiping parties." At all times, never far from any man was his pipe, as they were all "great tobacco-smokers," and never far from any gathering of women was a tea kettle, as they were "great tea drinkers."

A common form of winter transportation was the cariole, a type of sleigh pulled by a dog team or horse and, in true Metis fashion, it was often decorated. Nineteenth-century artist Paul Kane wrote: "The cariole is intended for carrying one person only; . . . the sides are made of green buffalo hide with the hair scraped completely off and dried, resembling thick parchment, this entirely covers the front part, so that a person slips into it as into a tin tub." Other writers referred to these sleighs as being "gay painted cariole[s]," decorated with "Russian bells on the dogs, and their harness is 'Frenchified' with beadwork and tassels." Kane also wrote that the Metis' dogs wore "gaudily decorated saddle-cloths of various colours, fringed and embroidered in the most fantastic manner, with innumerable small bells and feathers producing a pleasing and enlivening effect." On their horses they put brightly decorated saddle cloths and belts with red, white and blue beading on a black ground. Another writer noted: "Beribboned and prancing horses, either ridden by swash-buckling young men, or harnessed to gaily decorated carrioles, enlivened the road through a settlement or the frozen river in winter." Trotting matches were common as was any chance to show the prowess and speed of one's horse.

Because Metis descendants of the voyageurs were competitive by nature, a chance for a friendly challenge was never overlooked. In the 1860s Dr. W. B. Cheadle described their competitiveness as vanity and said it was one of the Metis' "besetting sins . . . they will leave themselves and their families without the common necessaries of life to become the envied possessors of a handsome suit, a gun, a horse or a train of dogs." Like other travellers who judged the Metis by European values, Cheadle did not understand that they had their own set of standards. Many had little in terms of material wealth. Alexander Ross records, for instance, that most

A dog train from Fort Garry at St. Paul, Minnesota, 1859. Courtesy Minnesota Historical Society, 67

houses in Red River had two rooms, "but they are all bare of furniture, and ornament never enters, except occasionally a small picture of the Virgin Mary, or a favourite Apostle, hung to the wall in a little round frame." Some Metis, however, sought to own a few flamboyant possessions as a way of expressing their individuality. Ross also relates the story of "a fellow with a showy horse and gay cariole" flying past him and a friend on "glib ice like lightning, with a lustre that threw us completely into the shade." The friend of Ross was forced to comment: "Who is that? . . . he must be a person of some consequence!" Ross explained that "this glittering Phaeton [sic] was not worth a shilling in the world."

The various mixed-blood newcomers who settled into the Red River community found themselves put into a class structure on the basis of occupation. Metis families who engaged in agriculture, trades or business were considered by the whites in the colony to have a higher status than those who hunted the buffalo. The latter were thought, however, to be of a higher rank than those who trapped and fished to survive and who came to the community only seasonally. But the Metis had a ranking system based on their own traditions and criteria and held the buffalo hunters in very high regard.

As the social class of the Metis population was variable, so were many other elements of their personal lives, especially their clothing, which reflected their mixed ancestry. Some wore fashionable European clothes, others dressed like Indians, or combined many elements of both cultures to create their own definitive Metis style. One writer noted that their attire was "notable mainly for its variety," and P. F. Tytler in 1854 offered a vivid description of what some of the men wore:

restrained by no Parisian code of fashion, the half-breeds dress in light blue cloth capotes, fastened round the waist with bright scarlet or parti-coloured worsted sashes. Very broad and conspicuous belts of the same colour, ornamented sometimes with white beads, cross their breasts and backs, to which they append powder-horns and shot-pouches. Leggins [sic] of variously coloured cloths, all more or less ornamented by the women, with beads or silk thread according to taste, clothe their legs. Moccasins, garnished with porcupine quills, dyed red, blue, and yellow, defend their feet, while their heads are decked with hats, caps, bonnets and nightcaps, or nature's own covering, all of which are covered profusely with tinsel hat-cords, gold and silver tinsel tassels, ribbons of every hue in the rainbow, and a good many more that the rainbow never displayed.

Many writers described male garments such as the blue capote, beaded moccasins and the red sash known now as a l'Assomption sash after the place in Quebec where many of them were made.

The wearing of a red sash was a tradition derived from the dress of the voyageur. Men also had beaded pouches and carried their rifles in ornamented covers. They wore a wide variety of hats of all shapes, sizes and materials — fashionable top hats bedecked with ribbons, fur caps made from a variety of pelts, broad-brimmed felt hats or a type of tam o' shanter. In the tradition of their Native ancestors, Metis women decorated those items to be worn by their husbands or that were made to be sold.

Women's costumes were described by the visiting Earl of Southesk as being dark and "not remarkable, though with

The spirit and strength of Metis tripmen and buffalo hunters is evident in this portrait. Their clothing varied, reflecting their individual character. But most wore a leather shirt, often decorated, while travelling in the summer or in heavy bush. Courtesy St. Boniface Historical Society

A portrait of Isabella Chalifoux, a Metis who married Francis Heron, a chief trader for the Hudson's Bay Company in 1835. Courtesy Glenbow Museum, NA 2365-72

much picturesqueness about the head-dress, which is sometimes a dark shawl or blanket worn as a hood, sometimes a crimson or yellow silk handkerchief." Ross noted that the shawls worn by the women were "chiefly of the tartan kind — all . . . of foreign manufacture." Young women often wore more brightly coloured shawls than their older relatives. For special occasions such as a dance Cheadle attended at Fort Carlton in 1865, women wore "bright-coloured skirts, showing the richly embroidered leggings, and white moccasins of cariboo-skin [sic], beautifully worked with flowery patterns in beads, silk and moose hair." They had more opportunities than other Native women to dress in fancy clothes, as dances, weddings and even church were occasions for wearing their "Sunday best." Metis women kept alive their Native heritage of costume decoration by using shells, seeds and quills to adorn clothing, which they adapted from European tradition, resulting in more tailored garments than those worn by Indians.

In the mission schools, girls were encouraged to do quill, bead or silkwork and were taught new embroidery techniques by the nuns, and these proved a significant influence on the designs and possibly the style of clothing that was produced. The use of floral embroidery seems to come from the tradition of the fur trader as well as from the churches and missions where the women observed painted designs, such as in the cathedral at Red River: "Over each column their [the nuns'] brushes created urns of various flowers, and from one column to the next was painted garlands of vividly coloured roses. . . . The native women, who enjoy silk-thread, bead and quill embroidery, came to copy these designs from the Cathedral." The women, many of them devout Catholics, were also influenced by the elaborate designs often found on priests' vestments.

Early Metis clothing was frequently made from hide (usually elk or deer) and was decorated with paint or quills. Very quickly, though, the Metis adapted these items to incorporate trade cloth, beads and silk thread brought by the Europeans. Using these more workable media, designs became even more elaborate, and any innovative or popular decorative motifs were shared by other women in the community as they discussed their work during their "gossiping parties."

Never afraid to experiment, women used a range of design elements and colours: sleeves were brightly adorned with red-and-white candy stripes, coats were painted with yellow, blue, red, black and pink in multicoloured patterning. Their designs also had a distinctive fluidity, and few elements stand alone without some line or connection to another part of the pattern. Their vibrant attitude towards life is reflected in the design elements and patterning, and the Earl of Southesk remarked upon "the gay fashion" of Metis clothing found in Saskatchewan, "where taste seems freer to indulge its fancies than in the graver regions of Fort Garry."

Beadwork was characteristic of that produced by Algonkian groups to which most of the Native ancestors of the Metis belonged. The same opposition of design is found on both Algonkian and Metis items — different designs on each side of a beaded bag. Native women, in turn, were influenced by Metis women to use floral patterns in their beadwork. Metis women are also thought by anthropologist J. Ewers to have "helped to introduce [to the Indians the use of] commercial dyes . . . a style of Indian dress resembling . . . that of white women . . . the braiding of hair . . . greater use of trade cloth . . . such household utensils as metal frying pans and spoons."

The Metis became an integral link to both worlds in all dimensions of their existence. The European cut of some of the coats the Metis women produced made them readily acceptable to the tastes of European visitors and souvenir hunters. Different, but not too foreign, these items along with Metis pouches, sashes and moccasins were collected by many who came to the regions where the Metis lived. Particular items of a certain style, size, material and decorative motif were probably commissioned from time to time by Europeans.

At the mission schools, which many Metis children attended, they learned more than beadwork and needlework. The ability to read and write helped to ensure employment for many apart from trapping and fishing. The religious doctrines of the churches that ran the schools were also taught to the children, entrenching more firmly their influence over the Metis.

Many of the Metis who had moved into the Red River colony never settled happily there. Some who participated in the northern hunts preferred to stay out on the prairie in winter camps: these men and their families were known as *hiverants*. Their small villages consisted of about "forty to fifty rough hewn, flat roofed cabins which, not withstanding their exterior, are warm and comfortable abodes. The shanties are facsimiles of each other, and in their erection the primitive style of architecture certainly predominates." Similar houses were found all over the prairies, with one or two families living in each house. "The doors are a rough hewn framework of wood over which is tightly stretched a buffalo parchment skin, the windows are of the same material, answering the two fold purpose of excluding the cold air, and serving as not a bad substitute for glass, in lighting up the capacious chamber." Floors were of earth or rough wood, and walls were often plastered

Top: A log hut in a Half-breed settlement, Wood Mountain, Saskatchewan, 1874. Courtesy Public Archives of Canada, C-81781

Left: A Half-breed hut in Wood Mountain, Saskatchewan, 1874. Courtesy Public Archives of Canada, C-12281

Right: The interior of a Metis house, drawn by Henri Julien and published in L'Opinion Publique, 1874. Courtesy Glenbow Museum, NA 47-10

with a mixture of buffalo hair and clay. On the walls was "an armoury of guns, powder horns and bullet bags; on the rafters a myriad of skins." Snowshoes, often decorated with paint and tufting, also hung on the walls of many houses. Often there were wooden trunks, a rude table and a few blackened kettles; all had buffalo robes covering the beds. Each house had a mud oven, which was replaced with an iron stove once the family became more established. Since the mud ovens were a fire hazard, wooden floors were usually plastered with mud to prevent sparks from starting a blaze.

In some of the more established *hiverant* villages, there was usually a large structure that served as the home and church of a travelling Oblate priest; there was also the house of a free trader.

Free traders who broke the monopoly of the Hudson's Bay Company had been part of life in the West since Guillaume Sayer was charged with illicit trafficking in furs with the Indians in 1849. He was brought to trial and found guilty, but was not punished because of strong opposition from his fellow Metis. As he left the court, one of the jurymen shouted, *"Le commerce est libre! Le commerce est libre! Vive la liberté!"* Among those who led the fight to break the trade monopoly of the Hudson's Bay Company was Louis Riel, Sr., the father of the man who would try twice in years to come to establish recognition of the rights of the Metis people in western Canada.

Free traders were often Metis who acquired furs and hides from trappers and traded them at Red River or joined a freight train to St. Paul, Minnesota.

The Red River cart used by the buf-

33

Half-breed traders, sometime between 1872 and 1875. Courtesy Public Archives of Canada, C-4164

falo hunters also became the trademark of the Metis freight trains, squealing their way along a variety of trails. The freighters' trek south was a family affair similar to that of the buffalo hunt and provided much the same atmosphere for camaraderie to develop amongst its members as the magnificent buffalo hunts. Every driver was expected to handle several carts at once and thus tied each ox to the cart ahead, allowing one man to drive as many as ten carts at a time. By 1856 trains of two hundred to three hundred carts, mostly owned and driven by Metis, were busy transporting about half of the goods sent from St. Paul to Red River. One writer upon looking back over a train saw:

[a] line extending far over the plain, the spare cattle following, and horses galloping about with very Cossack looking prickers [riders] after them, and the train winding its way, like a great snake, coming along very slowly, and then, when it got near enough, to hear the carts which, at a distance, sounded not unmusically, and then the lowing of the cattle, and the songs and voices of the men, until they at last got too near, and then it was bedlam again.

From Red River, the trains of carts hauled furs, pemmican, dried buffalo meat, moccasins and "skin garments fashioned by skilled Indian hands and worked with beads or porcupine quills" to St. Paul. On their return north, they brought with them groceries, tobacco, liquor, dry goods, ammunition and farm implements, as well as luxury goods such as window glass and even pianos.

The lifestyles of Metis freighters, tripmen and free traders were threatened in

1859 by the arrival of steam transportation in the Red River region. Hunters were also troubled, for the buffalo began to disappear from the eastern plains in the late 1860s. By the 1870s the herds were beginning to thin out all over the prairie region because of the greater take of hides for fur traders on the Missouri, overkilling by sport hunters and large hunts by the Metis. These disturbing developments, along with the winds of change that were coming from Canada at about the same time, were to seriously affect the lives of all Metis on the plains.

◇ ◇ ◇

At the time of Canadian Confederation, Prime Minister Sir John A. Macdonald dreamed of a nation that stretched from sea to sea, and in 1869 pressured the Hudson's Bay Company into relinquishing its lands to Canada, in return for a significant amount of land and a cash settlement of £300,000. This had a great effect on the Red River colony, for there had already been a steady trickle of settlers from Canada into the settlement, some of whom had begun to pressure for annexation to Canada. The dominant population, however, was still Metis, and they did not want any change in the North-West without their participation and consultation. At about that time, it was estimated there were 10 000 people in Red River, of whom only 1600 were white settlers.

Problems soon arose when the Canadian government sent a team of surveyors to the Red River area in the summer of 1869, before the new dominion had legally taken possession of the colony. To complicate matters, the township system of surveying square lots was being used, whereas many Metis lived on narrow lots fronting on rivers; they were also afraid of losing their homes, to which they did not possess official title.

In the tradition of his father, the young Louis Riel stopped the government party as it attempted to survey across the land of his friend, André Nault. He further organized a blockade to prevent the newly appointed lieutenant-governor, William McDougall, from arriving at the colony prior to the transfer of the territory. By stopping McDougall, Riel and the Comité National des Métis were attempting to "force the Canadian Government to negotiate with the half-breeds the terms of their entry into Confederation." Riel also convinced the English Half-breeds to side with the French Metis in their stand against the government, for though the English Half-breeds had strong ties to Upper Canada through their common language, Protestant religion and agricultural way of life, they, too, were in danger of losing their lands.

Tensions continued to mount as the Metis, led by Riel, resorted to drastic action to emphasize their demands. They seized Fort Garry, the centre of the Red River settlement, and set up a provisional government. This was the beginning of the Red River insurrection. The provisional government drew up a list of demands including, among other things, an elected legislature, representation in the Canadian Parliament, official status for both French and English languages in the courts and legislatures, and an economic plan to secure the future of the Metis people. These were to be presented to Ottawa by a spe-

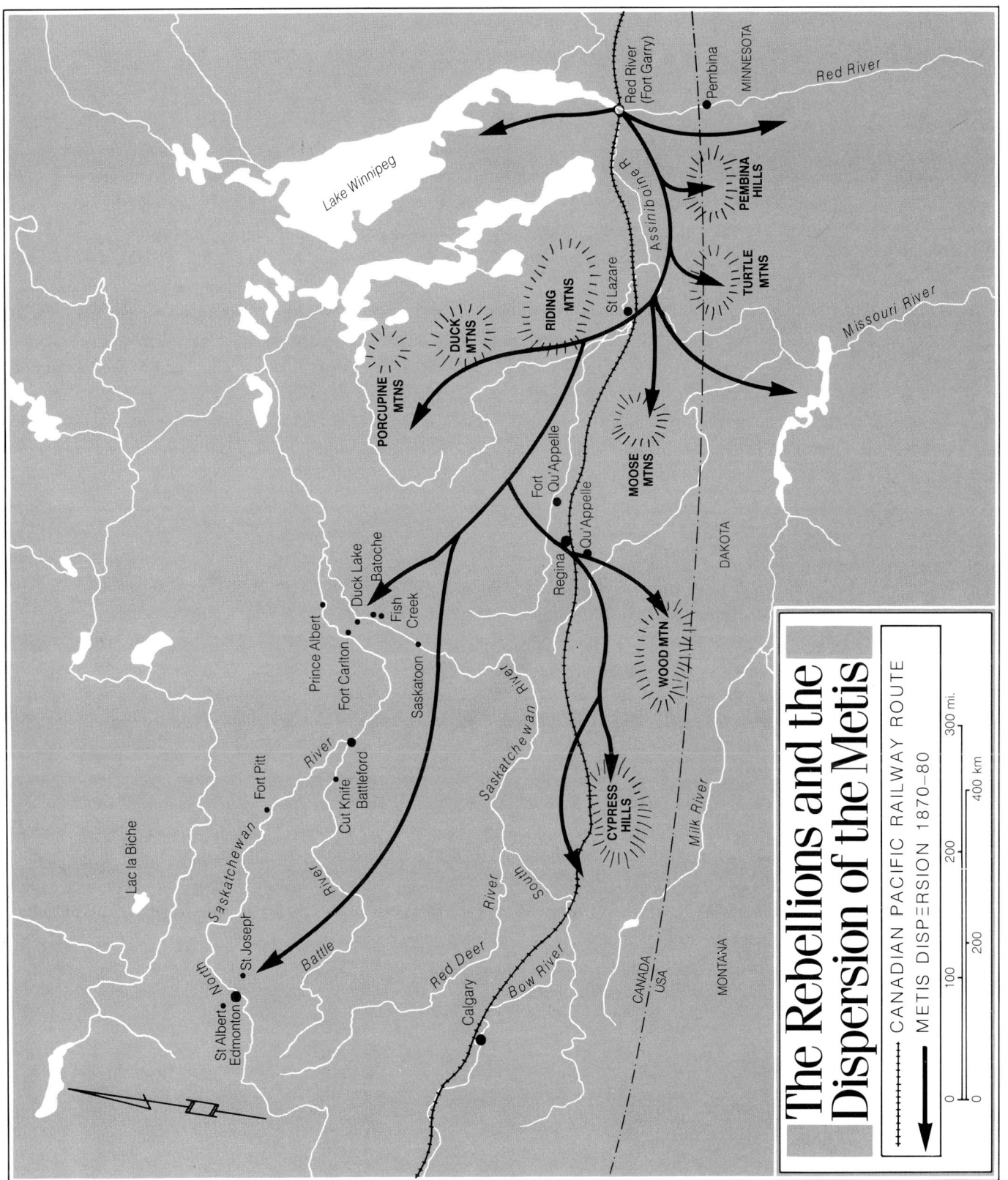

Louis Riel (middle row, 3rd from left) and his council in Red River circa 1869. Courtesy Glenbow Museum, NA 1039-1

cial delegation from the colony.

A peaceful settlement in Red River appeared to be forthcoming when controversy arose over Thomas Scott, an Orangeman from Ontario. After being arrested at Fort Garry by Riel in the fall of 1869, Scott escaped and attempted to raise a force against Riel and his followers. His cause met with little support from most residents of Red River and a short time later he was re-arrested. He continued to be an unruly, belligerent prisoner, and after an incident in the jail, he was tried and sentenced to death by the provisional government. Riel, as leader of that government, allowed the sentence to be carried out on 4 March 1870. His decision has been questioned by many since that fateful day, as it had long-lasting repercussions for the Metis.

Although the execution of Scott angered the Canadian government, Parliament passed the Manitoba Act in July 1870; it contained most of the items requested by the Metis, as well as asserting their land rights and assuring the continuation of a bilingual and confessional school system.

The Orangemen of Ontario demanded Riel's execution for the murder of

Thomas Scott, but Prime Minister Macdonald compromised on a sentence and banished him to exile. Riel fled to the United States ahead of the troops that were coming to put down the insurrection, but he was not forgotten by his followers and was elected to the House of Commons twice during his exile.

Racial biases had existed in the colony before the events of the winter of 1869–70 and were aggravated by the actions of the mixed-blood people against the Canadians and their government. The free, more mobile lifestyle of the French Metis population, along with their strong cultural identity, probably provided a buffer against some of the racism and resentment directed against them. In addition, many of them left the colony immediately following the troubles of 1870 to avoid such problems. As the number of white Canadian settlers increased, the English and Scottish Half-breeds who remained in Red River began to suffer more from racist attitudes. The Alexander Ross family, for example, was established and prosperous but suffered from racial prejudice because of their Native ancestry.

John Norquay, a Scottish Half-breed, rose to become premier of Manitoba from 1878 to 1887, but even he was not immune from racial slurs: "an annoyed member of the opposition hurled a taunt at the premier during a legislative session, saying 'It's the Indian in you.'" Norquay, who had stood apart from Riel during the insurrection, recognized the separateness of those who shared his same ancestry and the divisions within the group, stating that "Metis people do not have to think alike." His loyalty remained always with his people, stressing that they must be good Canadians first, though they must not lose pride in their heritage.

André Nault (left) and Ambroise Lepine (right) both joined with Riel in the 1869–70 insurrection. This photograph was taken in their later years, circa 1923. Courtesy Glenbow Museum, NA 4267-4

Many of the French Metis who left Red River after 1870 went to the North-West Territories (which included present-day Saskatchewan and Alberta), while others went to the United States, to Montana and the Dakotas, where they continued hunting buffalo, along with some farming, trapping and freighting. Some of their *hiverant* camps, though occupied only seasonally, became more established settlements as the years passed, with people placing a great reliance on large vegetable gardens of potatoes, turnips, cabbages and onions. These people still followed the buffalo, however, and as long as there were herds on the plains, the Metis tenaciously clung to being seasonally mobile to continue the pemmican trade. The Catholic priests continued to move with their "flocks" but were always encouraging them to become more settled.

The Sutherlands were a prominent Metis family in Red River in the 1870s. William Richard Sutherland (front row, 2nd from left), was deputy sheriff of the colony. Courtesy Glenbow Museum, NA 2365-77

In the hope of extinguishing Metis aboriginal titles to the land, the Manitoba Act of 1870 alloted 1 400 000 acres (567 000 ha) to families of all mixed-blood residents of the Red River colony. In addition, the allotment was expected to encourage the Metis to become large-scale farmers and to establish a settlement base in the West that would lessen the threat of annexation by the United States.

Distribution of the land did not begin until 1873, and initially, an allotment of 140 acres (57 ha) was given only to the children of Half-breeds who could prove residence in Manitoba at the time of the transfer of the Hudson's Bay Company lands to Canada. Establishing residency on 15 July 1870, the date of transfer, was a problem because a number of the Metis residents of Red River had been away on the buffalo hunt. In 1874 the government gave the heads of families 160 acres (65 ha) of land or $160 per adult. Later still, the allotment was changed to 240 acres (97 ha), and all other allotments were cancelled. Finally, by 1879, all the land set aside for the Metis had been given away, but many mixed-bloods were still coming forward to register for land. Confusion reigned. When the rules were changed, some Metis had their land taken away and given to new settlers. They were then given title to new pieces of land, which had to be cleared and upon which

they had to build new homes. At times, families that had left for the buffalo hunt returned to find that their homes had been given away. With such chaos, it is not surprising that many Metis gave up and joined their relatives farther west, where they had less government intervention in their lives. As they settled on the prairies, some of these people adopted the lifestyle of their maternal relatives. Many of them eventually signed treaties and accepted Indian status.

During this time, the whiskey trade began to flourish in the West. Demoralized and poverty stricken by the declining fur and buffalo resources, and frustrated by the government's failure to fully recognize their land claims, the Metis fell victim to the ravages of alcohol and the unscrupulous tactics used by many traders to secure buffalo hides from them.

Fearful for their lives and future as a result of the influx of settlers into the West with the coming of the Canadian Pacific Railway, the Metis of the North-West Territories firmly stated their concerns. In 1873 they petitioned the Canadian government for recognition of their claims as had been given the Manitoba Metis in 1870. The petitions arose from a local council set up by the Metis. Many of the laws passed by the council mirrored those of the buffalo hunt, but others reflected the European heritage of

Left: Members of the Lepine family, 1880s. Their dress and demeanour suggests an attitude and prosperity quite different from the "gay idleness" attributed to French Metis by European authors. Courtesy Glenbow Museum, NA 2631-7

Right: Mrs. Mary Thomas, circa 1870, a Metis woman who was the great-grandmother of Premier Peter Lougheed of Alberta. Photograph by Notman and Sandham, courtesy Notman Collection, McCord Museum

Facing page: Mixed-bloods in Manitoba in 1873–74. The clothing worn by the adults includes many Native and white elements, certain components of which became particularly identified with the Metis. Note the sash worn by the man on the right, and the garters on the man on the left. Courtesy Public Archives of Canada, C-79636

This page: Half-breeds near Maple Creek, Saskatchewan, 1884. Note the fringed capote worn by the man on the right. The style of his capote is typical of those worn by Metis on the northern plains in the late nineteenth century. Courtesy Public Archives of Canada, PA-50787

the Metis and the clergy who helped to structure the council.

Gabriel Dumont, the elected leader of the council, operated a ferry near Batoche at what became known as Gabriel's Crossing, ran a small store and also farmed a small plot of land. When not busy with all of this, he functioned as a contractor, organizing Metis labour crews to construct roads, mail stations, telegraph lines and cart-trail improvements. Dumont later became Riel's military strategist and is remembered by many of his people as a great leader, businessman and diplomat.

The Metis began to feel even more threatened by 1878, when a stream of Ontario settlers moved to the Prince Albert area following the promotion campaigns of the CPR, the Canadian government and land speculation companies. Metis requests were repeated through petitions to the government. While receipt of the petitions was recognized, and changes were made to the Dominion Lands Act in 1879 to include the Metis resident in the North-West Territories, nothing was actively done until early 1885. Integral to the question of a land rights settlement was the nature of the land surveys. As in the Red River colony, these were based on the township system and cut across the established lands of Metis who had followed their tradition of living on narrow lots that faced onto rivers.

Without question, the land issue was the main concern of the Metis population, but they also petitioned the government for a French-speaking magistrate for the region, the appointment of some Metis to the territorial council, subsidized schools and assistance to help them become established as farmers.

Left: Gabriel Dumont circa 1880. Courtesy Glenbow Museum, NA 1177-1

Right: An advertisement for Gabriel Dumont's ferry service at Gabriel's Crossing, published in the Saskatchewan Herald, 1880. Courtesy Glenbow Museum, NA-1829-5

Finally, in January 1885, the federal cabinet authorized an enumeration of the mixed-blood population in the North-West Territories, with the intent of eventually making land allotments. But to the frustrated Metis of central Saskatchewan, the government's action came too late and was not decisive enough, with no firm commitment as to what form the final settlement would take.

Initially, the English- and French-speaking mixed-blood people, along with some of the white settlers in the area, were united in their fights against the Canadian government. At a meeting on 23 May 1884, they decided to call on Louis Riel, who had achieved so much for his people at Red River in 1869 and 1870. The English Half-breeds did not totally support this suggestion, but they were overruled by the French Metis and those white settlers present.

A delegation consisting of Gabriel Dumont, Michel Dumas and Moise Ouellette, who were all French Metis, and James Isbister, an English Half-breed, set off for Montana to find Louis Riel. Riel, however, was a different man from the one they had known fifteen years earlier: after spending time in insane asylums in Quebec, where he had been diagnosed as suffering from

"'folies de grandeurs' or delusions of grandeur," he had become a fanatical Roman Catholic who saw himself as a new prophet. In Montana, where he taught school at St. Peter's Mission, Riel had married and had fathered two children, neither of whom lived beyond middle age nor had any descendants. Riel had joined the struggle for the rights of Metis and Indian people in Montana, aligning himself with the Republican party. It was at this time that the four Metis arrived from Saskatchewan to ask for his help in their conflict with the Canadian government. The return of Riel in 1884 provided a rallying point for some of the Metis. Initially, he tried to approach the government through petitions and meetings. When these were unsuccessful, he felt forced to take the same action that he had taken at Red River in 1869, and he established a provisional government at Batoche on 19 March 1885. Days later, the government in Ottawa sent troops under the command of Maj. Gen. Frederick Middleton to stop Riel. The problems in the North-West took on a much more threatening tone, and Gabriel Dumont was put in charge of military strategy for the Metis. Rumours of impending war flew across the prairies.

Left: Xavier Letendre dit Batoche, a prosperous businessman, left Red River for the Metis community of St. Laurent. He started a ferry service and a store at what later became known as Batoche. Courtesy Saskatchewan Archives Board, R-A 12, 116

Right: The house of Xavier Letendre, used as a headquarters by Riel in 1885. Courtesy Saskatchewan Archives Board, R-A 82

A Metis man, wearing a decorated jacket, who was a scout for the North-West Mounted Police circa 1885. Photograph by Fred A. Russell, courtesy Kalamazoo Public Museum

Many Metis were better off than the Indians who had been moved on to reserves, where poverty and starvation had become common by the early 1880s. Frustrated in their attempts to have the seriousness of their situation recognized by the Canadian government, some Indians, in concert with the Metis, finally resorted to armed resistance. At Duck Lake on 26 March 1885 the Metis clashed with the North-West Mounted Police and Prince Albert volunteers. Casualties were not heavy, and the Metis won the first battle of the North-West Rebellion. At Fish Creek on 24 April, the Metis battled the Canadian troops to a draw. The final battles were fought at Batoche from 9 May to 12 May. Although Middleton defeated the Metis at Batoche, they were not easily routed: greatly outnumbered, at times disorganized and with very limited arms, they kept the general and his men at bay for four days. About two hundred to three hundred Metis participated in the engagements, with an uncertain number being killed, though the estimated number of deaths was a hundred Metis and Canadians.

After the Metis defeat at Batoche, Gabriel Dumont and other leaders fled to the United States, but Louis Riel refused

to run and surrendered to Major General Middleton on 15 May 1885.

When the size of the entire mixed-blood population of the West is taken into consideration, a relatively small number actually participated in the rebellion. Many of the English Half-breeds around Batoche did not support the military actions of Riel and Dumont, and the French-speaking Metis at St. Albert actually formed a mounted rifle company to support the government forces.

Some Metis who had initially supported Riel wandered off at the time of battle. It was in keeping with the individualistic character of the Metis people, historically and even today, that in the end, they would reject an attempt at an all-encompassing authority.

Riel was found guilty of treason at his trial in Regina in the summer of 1885 and was sentenced to be hanged, in spite of a recommendation of leniency. He was executed on 16 November 1885.

Argument continues as to whether Riel should have died on the gallows, and there are those who believe he should receive a posthumous pardon. Some of the arguments are based on the facts, but others stem from the heart. Riel, despite his failings and questioned motives, stood for his people, who had legitimate complaints about the way they had been treated by the Canadian government.

The resistance of 1885 achieved far less for the mixed-blood population of the North-West Territories than had the Red River insurrection of 1869–70. The year 1885 was the beginning of a long period when the descendants of the strong, independent buffalo hunters of the plains and the fearless voyageurs of the fur trade were to suffer the pain and agony of prejudice, poverty and rejection. These misfortunes were what often served to unite the Metis, however tenuously, in their continued struggle for recognition and justice.

Left: The trial of Louis Riel (standing in box) in Regina, 1885. Courtesy Glenbow Museum, NA 1081-3

Right: Louis Riel in 1884. Photograph by C. A. Zimmerman, courtesy Glenbow Museum, NA 2631-2

An Expressive Individuality: Personal and Household Items

A number of Metis men were expert woodworkers because of the need to provide furniture in the European tradition for their homes. They also made their own means of transportation, from York boats and Red River carts to carioles and snowshoes. Many had the finely honed skills necessary to make fiddles.

Metis women, like pioneer women on the prairies, made braided rugs to add to the comfort of their homes. By decorating household and personal items such as pipebags, gun sheaths and tea cozies with needlework, beadwork and quillwork, they added touches of colour and beauty to their lives.

2

3a

50

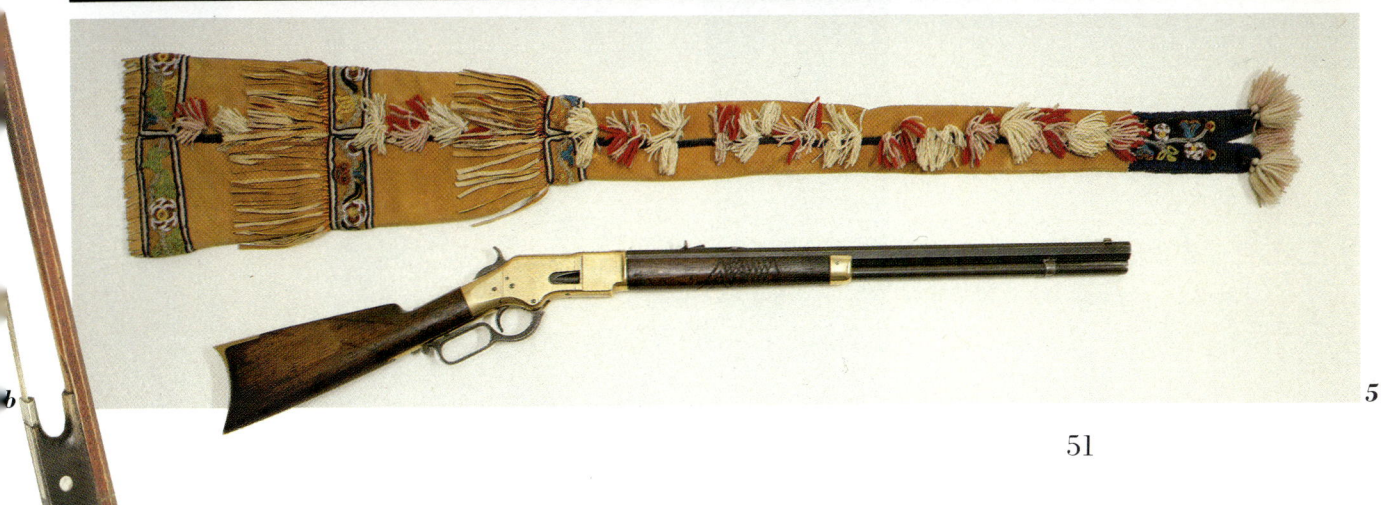

51

1. *Many Metis were devout Roman Catholics and often adorned their homes with religious items of various sorts. This coloured lithograph, a representation of* The Holy Grave of Mary, *is housed in a rough-hewn, handmade frame, which has been covered with a tarlike substance. Courtesy Glenbow Museum, AR 185*

2. *Although the tradition of smoking was a common link among all Metis, the types of pipes they smoked took many forms and were as divergent as their individual characters. Equally varied in form and design were the pipebags in which men carried their pipes. Courtesy Glenbow Museum, (pipebag, left) AT 2641; (pipebag, right) AT 2501; (pipes, top to bottom) AR 23, AR 10, AR 11, AR 24, AR 25, AR 22, AP 1006*

3. *Fiddle (a) and bow (b). Before commercially produced fiddles became readily available, many Metis made their own. Hudson's Bay Company records show "fiddle strings" as a commonly purchased item. In later years, however, most Metis purchased their fiddles — funds were somehow always available to obtain such an important item. Courtesy Glenbow Museum, (fiddle) C 11986a, (bow) C 11986b*

4. *The use of this type of pad saddle, often beautifully decorated, was possibly popularized across the West by the Metis of the nineteenth century. Courtesy National Museum of Man, V-B-424*

5. *Gun sheaths, decorated with beadwork, embroidery or quillwork, were used by many Metis, particularly those in the northern regions of western Canada. To a Metis, his rifle — which often exemplified the resilience of the Metis spirit in the extent of modification and repair that guaranteed its continued use — was unquestionably his most prized possession. Courtesy Glenbow Museum, AC 335*

6. *Firebags were a common personal possession of Metis. On this one, the flower jug, which seems to lack logic of placement in the overall design, is undoubtedly a European-inspired idea. The bag was made in Red River, Manitoba, by a Metis woman. Courtesy Haffenrefer Museum of Anthropology, Brown University, 57-453*

7. *This pristine example of a wall pocket, an item commonly found in Victorian homes, was collected by a Hudson's Bay Company factor at Norway House, Manitoba, in the mid-nineteenth century. He also left thirty pairs of never-worn moccasins in his estate. These items had probably been made for sale to the Hudson's Bay Company by Native and Metis women who lived around the post. The meticulous needlework, which incorporates European design elements, is typical of the work attributed to Metis women. Courtesy Glenbow Museum, AR 235*

Chapter Two

Change & the Struggle to Survive
1885 to 1920

Those who died on the battlefield were not the only casualties of the North-West Rebellion of 1885. To some historians, the events of 1885 spelled an end to any sense of Metis national unity: "Already undermined by the decline of the fur trade and disappearance of the buffalo, demoralized by racial abuse and religious bigotry ..., Metis national unity suffered its final blow in the flight into exile of Gabriel Dumont and the ... execution of Louis Riel."

The Metis rebellion also had far-reaching effects on the nation as a whole. Because so many Metis were of French ancestry, tensions between the French and the English increased and shook the foundations of Canadian unity. English Canadians viewed the rebellion as an insurrection against the government by Indians and Half-breeds led by the French, Roman Catholic murderer of an Ontario Orangemen. French Canadians saw Riel as leading the French in the struggle against English domination. Yet, in a roundabout way, Riel helped to save the dominion — and the CPR — by his actions. During the rebellion, the uncompleted railway had been used to send troops and supplies into the territories; for this reason, Macdonald was able to justify the use of government funds to keep the CPR construction going. In the words of CPR President W. C. Van Horne, "the company [CPR] ought to erect a monument to Riel as its greatest benefactor."

The rebellion had threatened Macdonald's dream of a nation that stretched from sea to sea by frightening potential settlers, who began to view the West as a dangerous place, but the completion of the Canadian Pacific Railway late in 1885 eased these fears and opened the West to settlement. Soon a steady stream of homesteaders were moving into the North-West, but because they were unaware of the history and culture of the Native population they saw only the destitution of the Indians and mixed-blood people and assumed it was their chosen lifestyle. Prejudice against the Metis and other Native groups increased. Not understanding that the Metis perceived the world differently and were either unconcerned by European standards of material comforts or lacked the means to acquire them, one nineteenth-century writer saw them only as "idle, dissipated, unreliable and ungrateful . . . possessing extraordinary powers of endurance . . . yet scarcely to be depended on in critical moments, superstitious and ignorant." Other newcomers made use of similar negative terms, focussing on the Metis' frivolous nature and presumed inability to settle down.

The Metis, however, were found at all levels of western society, not just as the buffalo hunters most frequently described by writers, nor did they always stand out as a different segment of the community, as discovered by an English lord who visited the Red River colony in the late nineteenth century.

According to Julian Ralph, who recorded the story, it occurred to the lord "while he was being entertained in a Government house . . . to inquire of his host, 'What are these halfbreeds I hear about? I should like to see what one looks like.' His host took the nobleman's breath away by his reply. 'I am one.'" The writer who recorded this incident went on to say that "there is no one who has travelled much in western Canada who has not now and then been entertained in a home where either the man or the woman of the household was of mixed blood, and in such homes I have found a high degree of refinement and

Pages 54/55: A French Metis with his wife and child at Fort St. John, 1895. Courtesy Provincial Archives of British Columbia

An unidentified Metis hunter on horseback circa 1890. Photograph by R. Randolph Bruce, courtesy Glenbow Museum, NA 22-33

Two Half-breeds in their winter camp, 1913. Courtesy Public Archives of Canada, PA-23042

Two mixed-bloods in southern Saskatchewan. Photograph by T. Weston, courtesy Public Archives of Canada (Geological Survey of Canada Collection), PA-50836

the most polished manners." This is a far cry from the description of all Metis as immoral, ignorant and rowdy, which cast a general pall over the Metis population of this era. The flamboyance of some Metis must have been seen as extravagant and unstable in the eyes of more dour and staid writers.

One gentleman who observed a group of Metis near the South Saskatchewan River noted that the intensity for life in all its aspects was part of the life of those Metis who lived out on the plains:

I have often been struck with the happy simple life that these people had. It has been my privilege to meet those freemen as they not inappropriately style themselves in every phase of their nomadic lives; in their devotions, in their family reunions at their own firesides, in their hours of toil and their seasons of recreation and I can honestly assert that I know a class of people, who perform the various duties of their position with such singleness of purpose: earnest and persevering in all their vocations, they have earned and fully deserve the measure of success that has crowned their labors.

He clarifies the point that he was speaking only of this community and that he had known of others that were not as

59

diligent. The same writer noted that the descendants of the French Metis who had moved out to Saskatchewan were "opposed to Indians, yet widely separated from the white man." As a result, they had a feeling of separateness from the rest of society and began to stress their political independence early. Other Metis who did try to integrate were often subtly isolated into a separate group through the prejudice quietly exercised against them. Some white people even suggested that mixed-blood people who married whites in an attempt to become part of the larger society "must feel rather ashamed to be seen with [their] 'black' relations."

Variations in lifestyle and customs increased even more as Metis began to leave Red River in greater numbers following the events of 1885. With the rush of white settlement in the West, new towns developed, attracting some Metis who often lived in shanties on the periphery, where they managed to eke out a living by working at odd jobs. To avoid discrimination from the white settlers,

Facing page: A camp of Metis workers who cleared brush for new settlers circa 1890. Their cart is a variant of a Red River cart. Courtesy Public Archives of Canada, C-1644

This page: A Hudson's Bay Company train of Red River carts in Calgary, 1888. Courtesy Glenbow Museum, NA 3489-42

Top: Metis freighters at the portage at Grand Rapids on the Athabasca River, 1899. Courtesy Glenbow Museum NA 949-83

Bottom: York boats like the one shown were used for river transportation for many years. Courtesy National Museums of Canada, 75-12353

Top: Metis men tracking a York boat up the Athabasca River, 1899. Courtesy Glenbow Museum, NA 949-141

Bottom: York boats, which often had crews of Metis men, continued to be used into the twentieth century. Courtesy National Museums of Canada, 75-12400

Two men, one a Metis, on left, packing up a slope at Pelican Portage, 1899. Courtesy Glenbow Museum, NA 949-86

some Metis changed their names to ones that would not reveal their ancestry, a practice that contributed to the decline in the numbers of identifiable Metis. Many moved farther west and north into the Peace and Mackenzie river areas. Some moved into northern Manitoba; others went south to the United States, joining relatives who had gone there following the events of 1870 in Red River. For several years groups of Metis wandered in the northern states until they finally settled in the central regions of Montana. Some of them moved to the foothills of the Canadian Rockies, where they eventually became absorbed into the general population. Others just roamed, looking for an area that would allow them the opportunity to live free and independent lives as they always had, on the land that was part of their very fibre and spirit.

In the typical Metis style of adapting to changing situations, their new homes were more rapidly built and less elaborate than those found in Red River. Generally, however, the size and finish of the houses varied according to the means and skills of the builders. Furniture was limited and very often handmade, but some people had a four-poster bed and a chest of drawers. From the tradition of creating furniture out of necessity, developed many fine Metis carpenters and cabinetmakers.

Many Metis women, like Mrs. Victoria Calihoo, worked very hard to keep their homes tidy. She lived in Lac Ste. Anne and records wiping her floors with moss after scrubbing them.

Diversity became the name of the survival game for most Metis in the next few decades; their lifestyle varied seasonally, encompassing some farming, freighting and labouring. As the West became more developed, many became homeless wanderers or squatted on land designated as road allowances, and their children had no access to schools. At this time diseases such as smallpox, tuberculosis and diphtheria were virulent among the Metis. The rampant whiskey trade also spelled destitution and death for many Metis, and it was often their own people, sometimes relatives, who promoted and sold the alcohol. When the wild food resources of the region diminished, the deplorable conditions worsened and whole families died of starvation and disease.

In the 1880s the thousands of buffalo skeletons that lay scattered around the prairie provided a temporary source of limited income for Metis who collected these bones, which were sent east to be pulverized and used for fertilizer. After the buffalo disappeared, some Metis, including those in the Qu'Appelle Valley, turned to hunting larger game such as deer for their regular subsistence until those animals were threatened by the spread of settlement and overhunting. Many Metis continued to hunt, trap and fish for a living, however, always on the edge of ever-encroaching settlements. Regulations passed by the government in the 1890s forbade the spring hunting of ducks and partridges, as well as fishing from October to December, and affected the survival of the Metis who relied on fish in the early winter and wild game in the early spring. Others managed to find work in other traditional Half-breed occupations as freighters for the Hudson's Bay Company and independent traders.

On the prairies it was common to see Metis wandering the countryside in rickety carts or wagons, picking up seasonal work wherever they could, mostly stacking hay or building fences for the new settlers in the region. In winter they survived by cutting wood and selling it to people in towns or on farms. In the early spring they hunted small animals for food and for their pelts. Some Metis eked out a living by hauling railroad ties at the rate of twenty cents a tie, averaging twenty to twenty-five ties per load per day, or took menial jobs at NWMP barracks in exchange for provisions and board; others found employment in large businesses such as the lumber companies that were developing in the region. Digging seneca root, which was used in the preparation of medicines, was another small source of income (though as late as the 1930s they received only a price of thirty cents per pound (250 g) after hours of backbreaking labour). Numbers of Metis could find no source of employment and were forced to go on relief, including the widows of those who had died in the rebellion.

Louie Calihoo, who left St. Albert during this time, described his own situation as the twentieth century approached:

I left my old home at St. Albert coming to Grande Prairie in September, 1896, with an outfit of four pack horses, looking for a new location at the same time I spent the winter here trapping. In the spring of the year 1896 we all moved to Bear Creek where the present town of Grande Prairie stands now. We camp there for the spring fishing. . . . I went on back home to move my family up. I moved just my family to Lesser Slave Lake. I put up hay there that same fall. I went back to St. Albert to get my cattle. I wintered there. In the spring of March 1898 the Klondike rush was on so I stop off there was a chance for making good money on carpenter work for no carpenters there then. At the same time I put some of my boys to school at Grouard for was no school up here. Then in the spring of 1899 I moved up here with all my outfit, horses, cattle and what little machinery I had. Sowed oats and barley in latter part of the summer there.

Three mixed-blood women circa 1907. The tartan shawls they are wearing were typical of those used by Metis women for several generations. Courtesy Glenbow Museum, NA 726-21

Fishermen, farmers, freighters, merchants, woodcutters, gold miners, carpenters, masons, trappers, boatmen — name the task and there were Metis who were performing it. As was typical of their heritage, they moved to where the action was. Throughout the territories, Metis could be found struggling or flourishing in many types of employment along rivers, lakes, railways and roads. This reinforces the essence of the Metis individual — his goals and aims were determined by his own priorities. To some, integration, not assimilation, into the new settled lifestyle of the territories was the goal; to others, it was to remain independent from the larger society. But even the poorest Metis had a sense of entrepreneurial spirit, and every potential employment opportunity to be found in the West was exploited by some member of the Half-breed population.

To all Metis, but particularly those who continued to live directly off the land, two items were of utmost importance to survival. One was a gun, the other a knife, and these were probably no farther away from a man at any moment than was his pipe. Many Half-breeds who lived in the hinterland had but one item of cutlery — a knife: "While the meat lasts, life is one long dinner. A child scarce able to crawl is seen with one hand holding a piece of meat, the other end of which is tightly held between the teeth, while the right hand wields a knife with which it saws away between fingers and lips till the mouthful is detached. We have never seen a native minus his nose, but how noses escape amputation under these circumstances is an unexplained mystery."

Guns and knives were kept in sheaths, which were often decorated both for personal pleasure and protection of the weapons. Guns owned by Metis were not sophisticated firearms for their time, and most of them who had fought in the 1885 rebellion had only smooth bore shotguns rather than rifles with which to defend themselves. But no matter what firearms they used, they were fine marksmen. Their rifles were known as the "short northwestern gun." As the Blackfoot did, the Metis were observed to file off the barrel leaving it but little longer than that of a horse-pistol. One old Metis was reported to have "an old flint rifle, a most extraordinary little implement so short and small, so bound up and mended with leather and brass-headed tacks, and altogether worn and weather-beaten, as to look like some curious antique toy."

In the more northern regions, Metis continued to use carioles pulled by dogs and always carried fancy whips with large woollen pompoms on the top to "prevent [them] from sinking from sight when dropped in the soft snow." The dogs were often dressed in elaborately decorated blankets called "tuppies," which were decorated with wool or silk on stroud.

But the most common item possessed by all Metis men was a pipe. Jockie Calder, the son of a Scottish factor and an Indian mother, was well known for his beloved pipe. A well-liked, honest man, he was never without it, and is remembered for the mixture he put in it — a combination of cheap tobacco and red willow bark, sprinkled with cheap perfume. He carried this mixture in a beaded pouch that hung from his belt, and the smoke could be smelled a mile away. Such a mixture, minus the perfume, was commonly smoked by Metis and Indians alike.

The clothing worn by Metis of this era still followed the traditions of old, though influenced by localized fashion trends, which were also known among most Native groups in Canada and at times played havoc with the supplies brought by traders, who found that certain colours of beads had fallen out of favour. And some of the variability found in Metis dress may well have been due to the dictates of fashion in conjunction with a definite personal taste. One such trend was noted by Ernest Thompson Seton, an early conservationist, on a canoe trip that took him through northern Alberta in 1907. At Fort McKay, Seton hired a Half-breed guide called Jiarobia, but his wife, who wished her husband to remain at home for a while, protested his entering Seton's employ. As a bribe to forestall her objections, Seton allowed her to select from the Hudson's Bay store "the finest silk handkerchief." To his amazement, "she turned from all the bright coloured goods and selected a large 'black' silk handerchief." Seton recorded: "the men tell me it is always so now; fifty years ago every

A group of Half-breeds at Buffalo Narrows, Saskatchewan, circa 1900. Courtesy Public Archives of Canada, PA-44552

woman wanted red things. Now all want black; and the traders who made the mistake of importing red have had to import dyes and dip them all."

Numbers of Metis created their own independent style, and Seton told the story of one woman who lived on the Alberta–Northwest Territory border in the early 1900s and was known to all around as the "social queen." She was very proud to point out that her door was "painted blue," even though it was the only paint to be found on the entire house. Inside, "on the walls snowshoes, fishing lines, dried fish in smellable bunches . . . , a musical clock that played with painful persistence the first three bars of 'God Save Our King.'" Everywhere else were rags, mud and dirt. Enunciating the fact very emphatically that she knew the ways of "ze Indian" and the ways of "ze halfbreed" but that she followed the ways of "ze white man," she proudly pointed to a pair of "Louis Quinze slippers and French corsets" that were hung up with a bunch of dried fish. "When she went shopping to the Hudson's Bay Company store she had to cross . . . a great open space; she crowded her brown bare broad feet into the slippers, then taking a final good long breath she strapped on

Top: The interior of a Metis hiverant cabin, circa 1910. Photograph by James K. Cornwall, courtesy Glenbow Museum, NA 1267-1

Bottom: The interior of a house in a Metis winter camp, 1913. Courtesy Glenbow Museum, NA 493-5

Jock and Duleau McDonald with their carioles and dog teams near Edmonton circa 1890. Courtesy Glenbow Museum, NA 1337-3

the fearfully tight corsets outside of all. Now she hobbled painfully across the open, proudly conscious that the eyes of the world were upon her. Once in the store she would unhook the corsets and breathe comfortably till the agonized return . . . was in order." This woman was also known to speak "like a white woman," calling her daughter "darr-leeng."

Another guide whom Seton hired was dressed in the "cast off garments of a white tramp," but despite his drab and tattered clothes, he wore a pair of brightly beaded moccasins. "However sordid these people may be in other parts of their attire," Seton noted, "they always have some redeeming touch of color and beauty about the moccasins which cover their truly shapely feet."

The needlework of Metis women was influenced by the mission schools, and one writer in the earlier twentieth century observed that "in practically every line, the work done by half-blood women and by native girls in the mission schools is far superior to purely aboriginal work . . . bead and silkwork are the principal methods of decoration . . . floral designs are the ones used." Perhaps some of the Metis competitive spirit, as well as pride in their skill and

Top: A Metis couple in a small sleigh, going to Lac la Biche for the New Year celebrations, 1895. Photograph from Caspar Whitney, On Snow-Shoes to the Barren Grounds, courtesy Glenbow Museum, NA 1185-4

Bottom: A Metis dance in the home of Mr. Firth, during the winter of 1908–09. Courtesy Glenbow Museum, NA 513-20

a sense of tradition, had a great deal to do with the high quality of work some of these women produced. Friendships of women who lived around posts or missions might also have led to some of the consistency of style found in Metis beadwork and embroidery.

Not all women, however, were fine needleworkers. In 1874 a friend of Alexander Morris, son of the lieutenant-governor of the North-West Territories and the Keewatin district, wanted to commission some silkwork. He had some difficulty getting it, "for there are but a few women who can do it nicely." He located six women who did fine work, but only three could complete it in time, and he was dismayed at how long it took them to finish. Obviously, he did not understand the extent of the work involved because he thought that six weeks was excessively long, though he conceded that the work may have been exceedingly tedious! The women were paid in cash for their labour after the supplies had been bought for them. The intended function of these pieces was unimportant to the Metis women; they were simply filling the needs of another market.

Metis and Native women who lived around settlements made decorated pillow cases, piano covers, picture frames, book covers and other such items for local white residents in return for some tea, sugar or a bit of flour. Although, initially, many pieces were commissioned, some were later used in Metis homes. Among other items created by the women were shelf decorations to be used in the home, or in local churches or convents.

Priests continued to play a major role in the life of the Metis as they had been doing since their early arrival in the West. To encourage the Metis to give up their wandering and become farmers, some priests refused to accept into their schools children whose families continued to move seasonally. In many cases, however, this action fuelled the smouldering fires that had been stirred during the 1885 rebellion, when the church had not supported Riel and his military actions.

Following the traditions of their ancestors, many of the Metis "were strict Sabbatarians. . . . The breeds maintained, with many white swear words for lack of strong talk in Indian, that they never knew Sunday work to end in anything but disaster, and . . . produced their cards." Often, they spent the day playing poker or an Indian hand game.

Other special days were kept according to both their European and Native heritage. St. Jean Baptiste Day, 24 June, was celebrated at Batoche for many years. Originally a religious celebration, it was highlighted by sports events and ended with a *feu de camp* and a feast. At times liquor became a problem and the attendants became somewhat rowdy, but local priests and police noted that this was generally out of character for most Metis. Native traditions that concerned the coming of age of children and seasonal rituals were also observed by some groups of Metis.

A number of Metis, however, began to deny their Native heritage and made an effort to fit into white society. To many whites, all Natives were Indians, and the Metis, being part-Indian, belonged on reserves; but Half-breeds were not always accepted by the Indians either.

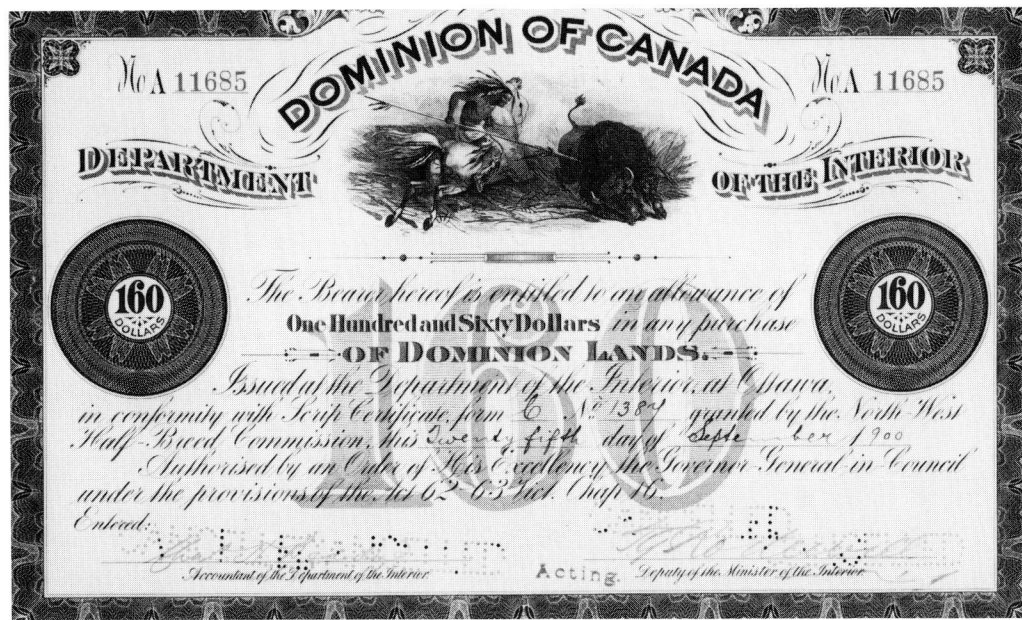

A land scrip certificate issued by the North-West Half-Breed Commission in 1900, entitling the bearer to an allowance of $160 on any purchase of dominion lands. Courtesy Glenbow Museum, NA 2839-18

Because they were not included in the treaty system, they were often considered a nonpeople by both groups. Although some Metis preferred to retain their own identity, which was separate from both groups, the government did not recognize their cultural difference.

The Half-breed population presented a problem, as many could not afford the land grants offered to new settlers nor were they entitled to reserve status. Yet, legally and morally, they had a claim to land. Prime Minister John A. Macdonald declared in 1885 that the "half-breeds . . . are whites" and must be treated the same as other Canadians, "as if they were altogether white." The events of 1885 forced the government to take seriously the rumblings coming from the North-West Territories, and the Street Commission was appointed in 1885 to implement land distribution to Metis on the basis of a government certificate called "scrip." The word "scrip" comes from the Latin *scription*, meaning "to write." In this context scrip was a provisional document that entitled the holder to receive something else, such as goods or land. To the Metis, scrip meant land.

There were two types from which the Metis could choose — money scrip and land scrip. Most Metis took money scrip: in 1885, 1710 money scrips were issued, but only 232 land scrips. In 1899 only 46 land scrips were taken and 1195 money scrips. Later, the Metis criticized the government for even offering money scrip in exchange for the extinguishment of their aboriginal title.

Issued in different dollar values, scrip looked like money and was, in fact, printed on paper from the Canada Bank Note Company. The Metis were given notes in values of $80, $160 or $240; money scrip could be exchanged for cash and land scrip for a block of land. When the government began the scrip program, it valued land at one dollar an

A scrip commission meeting at the Hudson's Bay Company post on Lesser Slave Lake, 1899. Courtesy Glenbow Museum, NA 949-18

acre (0.4 ha); thus, a scrip note for land valued at $160 could be exchanged for 160 acres (64 ha). Later, when land values increased, the scrip notes became worth less.

Many Metis were allowed to retain title to some of the river lots that they had established in Alberta and Saskatchewan, but the concept of "owning" land was not critical to some of them; what they desired was the freedom to "live on" the land. Numbers of Halfbreeds continued to squat on random lots, not seeing the need to establish a permanent claim to any one place.

Throughout the land settlement program, several scrip commissions travelled to the North-West. Essentially, these were royal commissions vested with the power to deal with claims "in the North West where Indian title had already been ceded." There were several of these, including the North-West Half-Breed Commissions of 1885, 1886 and 1887; the Scrip and Treaty Commission of 1899, and the Scrip Commission of the early 1900s. Advertisements in newspapers and postings in church halls, land offices and trading posts announced the forthcoming arrival of the commissions.

When a scrip commission arrived in an area, it became "the biggest social event of the year. . . . Every merchant

A land scrip certificate, face value $240, made out to Jean Baptiste Forcier on 23 June 1894. Courtesy Glenbow Museum, NA 2839-4

arrived with his goods for the . . . circus or fair." The *Edmonton Bulletin*, on 4 July 1885, described the sitting of one commission: "The town had flush times during these four days. The stores and saloons reaped a regular harvest, horses and cattle changed hands at lightening [*sic*] speed and at good figures and the spring horse race absorbed whatever money could not conveniently be blown in any other way." The next week, when the commission moved to St. Albert, an observer reported: "A dozen beer saloons adorn the grounds, and a lively trade is done in everything that can be sold or bought. Horse and dog racing and betting have been rife all week, but it is impossible to file a report of the numerous events, whose importance lay in the fact that Edmonton and St. Albert bet against each other on them."

Not everyone who should have appeared was able to do so, however. News of a commission did not necessarily penetrate to the far corners of the territories where a lone hunter might be located, but many people did get to the hearings to present their claims. Because land could not be distributed until treaties had been signed, the Metis became instrumental in encouraging Indians to take treaty, thus relinquishing their rights to the land.

When a Metis came before a commission, he had to establish that he was of Native heritage but had not previously accepted treaty. The commission could decide to allow his claim, delay it for consideration in Ottawa or disallow it. Metis who spoke only French or a Native language feared it would be embarrassing and humiliating to appear before stuffy gentlemen from Ottawa who conducted all the proceedings in English, and so did not put forward claims at all. Moreover, to illiterate Metis, the paperwork process, necessary affidavits and other elements of red tape were confus-

Facing page: Throughout his tenure in the West, Father Lacombe worked diligently to ensure a secure future, based on agriculture, for the Metis. Courtesy Glenbow Museum, NA 1358-1

ing, and they considered it even more ridiculous that they should have to go through this process when they knew the land had been theirs to begin with.

A number of people of Native ancestry were eligible for either treaty or scrip. Those who took treaty found their privileges and legal standing changed drastically, affecting their identity for years to come. They became wards of the government, which assumed responsibility for their care. Although most often inadequate, this care included health services, education and rations. When scrip was taken, the government assumed no further obligation, and the recipients were expected to become independent farmers.

The clergy were a major influence on the issue of who sought scrip and who applied for treaty. They encouraged people to take treaty rather than scrip, partly because missions received government grants based on a per capita enrolment in their schools, which were exclusive to Treaty Indian children. Also, they often felt that some Native people were not ready for full citizenship. Because many Metis had witnessed the poverty and deprivation suffered by those who had taken treaty, they chose the more prestigious scrip. Taking treaty meant being confined to reserve lands, and they wanted to be free to hunt and travel where they wished. Many people who had taken treaty later withdrew in order to take scrip.

Although land scrip was supposedly designed to prevent speculation, the government did little to discourage land speculators who followed scrip commissions. The speculators were an integral part of the melee and frivolity that the *Bulletin* described as accompanying commission visits. Those Metis who took land scrip were encouraged by the speculators to sell at prices that may have been slightly higher than money scrip was worth but that were still lower than speculators or white farmers would have had to pay for the same piece of land. The government's primary concern was to see western land developed, which required an agricultural settlement base. Most Metis had shown a distinct disinclination towards farming beyond their own immediate needs, which may explain the government's unwillingness to take any action against the speculators, even allowing speculation firms to openly advertise in newspapers and dominion land offices to attract settlers.

Speculators would travel to an area ahead of the commission and obtain power of attorney to appear at the hearings on behalf of illiterate Metis; sometimes the speculators never returned to deliver the money or land scrips owing to the Metis. Those who did receive payment often got much less than the face value, sometimes as little as fifty per cent. Some of the more prominent scrip speculators included the Imperial Bank of Canada, Bank of Montreal and Bank of Nova Scotia, as well as private banks and individuals. Many of them were allowed to establish accounts with dominion land agents and the Department of the Interior to allow for easy transfer of Metis land titles.

One reason why Metis took money scrip was that the land allotment offered was not large enough for hunting and trapping. Furthermore, many of these people were destitute and needed money immediately for food and clothing. When an attempt was made to end money scrip distribution in 1899, the Metis protested. In their eyes a lump sum payment was more desirable to satisfy their immediate needs.

Many other problems were inherent in the land scrip system. For instance, a Metis who received his scrip at Batoche had to travel over 700 miles (1120 km) to the dominion land office in Calgary to locate his piece of land. This trip may have cost him more than the scrip was worth, and it was often three years before he received actual patent to his property. In addition, farming was a risky business, and many Metis did not have the money to invest in equipment and improvements. However, since they were entitled to obtain scrip for minors, some people were able to raise enough capital through the sale of their children's scrip to establish farms. Another difficulty arose from the fact that the only lands available to Metis were those opened for homesteading, and often they did not receive patent to lands on which they were already living. They might even receive an allotment miles away from family and friends. Prejudice was another problem, as some of the new settlers were hostile to Natives, and many Metis disposed of their land promptly upon receipt to avoid facing the discrimination that was certain to be directed at them.

While the scrip commissions brought the opportunity to develop a successful farm or a business to some Metis, to most they brought poverty, destitution and desperation. People continued to wander the prairie region into the twentieth century in search of a life that would

give them stability yet allow them to retain their independence.

Canadian government efforts to turn the Metis into large-scale farmers proved to be unsuccessful, as providing land through the scrip program had not encouraged many to settle on farms. However, little consideration was given to the fact that their lack of success as large-scale farmers may have been the result of economic factors and problems inherent in the scrip program.

A further attempt was made to encourage the Metis to accept farming by Father Albert Lacombe, an Oblate priest. He petitioned the government for assistance to establish a farming colony on "a land reserve which could not be sold or taken away by fraud and on which the Metis could become economically self-sufficient." The Metis were not consulted on the planning of this colony, and Father Therien, who was to become its manager, recorded that if they did not succeed, then the population could be replaced by French Canadians. It appears his prime motive was not so much to help the Metis as to ensure a Catholic presence in the West.

On 28 December 1895 the federal cabinet passed an order-in-council establishing the colony of St. Paul des Métis on a twenty-one year lease of land adjacent to the Saddle Lake Indian Reserve in present-day northeastern Alberta. Although a grant of $2,000 was given for seed grain and equipment, it was withdrawn in 1897. In 1899 the Grey Nuns opened a boarding school, using what precious money there was for the construction of a school building.

The Oblates doubted that the colony would ever be successful with only Metis residents and began to encourage settlement by French Canadians, who were thought to be model farmers. There were successful Metis farmers who were not allowed to move to the colony, though they could possibly have served as better and more familiar models. Only fifty Metis families ever came to St. Paul des Métis, where they were given title to only eighty acres (32.4 ha), exactly one-half the standard homestead allotment. Consequently, it was almost impossible for them to make a financial success of their individual farms.

In August 1908 the board of management of the colony recommended that the lease be terminated and that the colony be closed. Because the status of the land granted to them had never been well defined, the Metis farmers were opposed to closing the colony. Their fears were justified, as later they had to fight to retain their claims to the land; some did succeed in keeping their farms, but others left the colony in search of work and subsistence. They scattered in many directions, joining other landless and jobless Metis wandering the countryside.

In 1905 Alberta and Saskatchewan, formerly part of the North-West Territories, became the eighth and ninth provinces to join the Dominion of Canada. As provinces, they accepted full responsibility for the citizens within their borders, and this included the Metis, who, following the issue of scrip, had been allowed access to the full rights and responsibilities of Canadian citizens. Unlike the Indians, they did not have the protection of a special status under federal legislation. Instead, they were subject to the individual legislation of

the three prairie provinces in which they lived. They now had to petition their respective provincial governments rather than approaching, as one body, the federal government for any action to improve their situation. Not until several decades later were the Metis to unite again to present a single voice demanding action to alleviate their plight.

Because scrip had denied the Metis any of the privileges of the ward status of the Treaty Indian population, they were often poverty stricken and unable to have access to schooling, health care and, most critically, land. Some managed to become integrated members of the community, but this was often at the price of denying their ancestry. At the same time, the differences in status between Indians and Metis drove a rift between them that still exists today. The Indians often saw the Metis as trying to gain access to the privileges they had; the Metis saw the Indians as relatives who had rights that they too wanted and felt they deserved because of their common ancestry.

As the first years of the twentieth century rolled by, the situation for many Metis did not improve. Then in 1914 came the First World War and the need for men to serve in Canada's fighting

Mrs. Robert Gladstone (née Zilda Jervais), a Metis woman, at the turn of the century. Her dress reflects strongly her European heritage. Photograph by Steele & Co., courtesy Glenbow Museum, NA 102-2

Members of the Moberley family, Metis, from the Jasper area of Alberta, circa 1900. Courtesy Glenbow Museum, NA 3187-17

St. Pierre and Adolphus Poitras, two Metis gentlemen, at St. Paul, Alberta, 1910. Courtesy Glenbow Museum, NA 3865-2

Alex Gladstone and Dan Nault, two cowboys at Pincher Creek, Alberta, circa 1900. Photograph by H. J. Pierrier, courtesy Glenbow Museum, NA 102-5

Mrs. Eliza Wood (née Kipling), a Metis war widow, Calgary, circa 1916. She is wearing her husband's military insignia. Courtesy Glenbow Museum, NA 2365-84

Many Metis names, such as Riel, Lepine, Nolin and Trottier, can be found on Canada's military Roll of Honour list, including that of

Private Patrick Riel, nephew of Louis Riel, killed in action . . . [in] France, January 16, 1916. "Paddy" Riel was a woodsman and trapper who depended upon the accuracy of his shooting for his livelihood. He enlisted with the 8th Battalion, Little Black Devils, the regiment which, thirty years before had stormed the Metis stronghold at Batoche. When a friend of Paddy's, a Scotch half-breed called MacDonald, was killed by shrapnel at Hyde Park Corner on January 9, 1916, Paddy swore to avenge his death by getting fifteen of the enemy. But six days later, Paddy himself was killed at Ypres, without managing to avenge the death of his friend.

forces. Being loyal Canadians, and seeing an opportunity to break the bonds of poverty and desperation, many Metis enlisted, offering to give their lives for a nation that had been questionably just to them. Exactly how many Metis enlisted may never be known as the nominal roll lists for the Canadian Expeditionary Force include only such information as name, next of kin, place and date of enlistment, and country of birth. Canada's own true sons, the Metis, were the least specifically identified, because to be born in Canada did not reveal whether or not a man was of Native ancestry.

More information is available about Treaty Indians who enlisted in the Canadian Expeditionary Force than there is for the Metis, though details are still sketchy. At the time the Indians signed treaties with the Canadian government, they were assured that they would not have to participate in any war effort in which Canada engaged. Soon after Canada became active in the war, however, recruiting offices opened unofficially on some reserves and many Indians enlisted. This patriotic effort on the part of the Indians, who were wards of the government and did not have the rights or responsibilities of citizens, drew special attention and was recorded in the annual reports of the Department of Indian Affairs. On the other hand, the Metis were viewed as having the responsibilities of any other citizen and were

expected to do their part for the war effort.

The performance of those who were of Native ancestry became part of the folk history of the war, for they were noted for their bravery and accuracy with their rifles. This stems from the pre-enlistment lifestyle, in which many were hunters, as well as from the heritage of the great buffalo hunt. Joseph Cosley, son of a French-Canadian trapper and his Cree wife, became a "sharpshooter" in the 113th Regiment and was credited with killing more than sixty enemy soldiers during the four-year conflict.

Unfortunately, the admiration that soldiers of Native ancestry earned on the battlefield was not carried over when they returned to Canada. Removed from the camaraderie and life-and-death situation of war, they became, again, relegated to the status of "dirty Indians or Halfbreeds." Many Metis veterans, who had experienced life and travelled far beyond the boundaries of their homes in the rugged regions of Alberta, Saskatchewan and Manitoba, left their communities to move to the rapidly growing urban centres on the prairies, in the hope of finding some of the advantages they had experienced during their service. Others stayed, warriors home from battle, and resumed their lives among family and friends.

Henry Nor'West, spinning a lasso, Red Deer area circa 1912. He later became a hero in the First World War for his exploits as a sniper. Photograph by Bell, courtesy Glenbow Museum, NA 1959-1

An Independent Style: Early Metis Clothing

Clothing made by Metis women for their men or as commissions or for sale was an unusual combination of their Native and European heritage. Although often European in style and cut, early garments were often fashioned of hide rather than cloth and also followed the Native tradition of fringes and adornment. Needleworkers used materials from both cultures: quills, beads and silk embroidery thread. The distinctive design elements were also drawn from their dual heritage: Cree geometric patterns, quilled rosettes (possibly an adaptation of the quilled discs worn by Indian men) and floral motifs derived from European influences. So distinctive was Metis floral embroidery that both the Sioux and the Cree called them the "flower beadwork people."

1

2a

2b

86

5

6

1. *Winter Travelling by Dogsled, a painting by Paul Kane, 1840s. All the elements in this painting — the clothing worn by the driver, the decorated cariole, the elaborate dog harnesses and blankets — are typical of those described as being worn and used by Metis of the era. Courtesy Royal Ontario Museum, 912.1.48*

2. *Front (a) and back (b) of one coat. Modelled on the narrow-waisted, broad-shouldered European coats of the 1840s, this piece is in the Metis tradition of elaborate, innovative decoration. It is highly unlikely that this coat was ever worn, given its pristine condition, even though the logic of its construction suggests that it was made to fit a particular individual. Courtesy Glenbow Museum, AR 295*

3. *This waistcoat is made in a style popular in the 1850s and displays the vibrant, flamboyant decoration used by many Metis craftswomen. The low position of the notch on the lapel suggests a lack of understanding of its function. Such misinterpretations were common on Metis variations of European tailored clothes. Courtesy Glenbow Museum, AR 243*

4. *This hide jacket was made by a Metis woman in the early twentieth century. The many floral elements and fine craftsmanship are typical of much of the work attributed to Metis artisans. Courtesy National Museum of Man, VI-Z-249*

5. *The Metis were known to wear a variety of headgear, ranging from top hats and peaked Glengarry caps to the fur hats that came from their Native heritage. Hats like this factor's cap were also worn by some Metis. It is similar in style to the smoking caps worn by gentlemen in the 1880s, but is made from deerhide and decorated in a manner common to much Metis embroidery. Courtesy Manitoba Museum of Man and Nature, H 4.12.116*

6. *L'Assomption sashes, as they are often called — after the name of the place in Quebec where many of them were made — are an enduring symbol of the Metis people. The sashes were traded extensively throughout North America by fur traders, and due to their intimate involvement in the trade, many Metis wore them as part of their regular attire. The sashes served a functional purpose, as often the key to an individual's trunk, in which his every possession was usually stored, was attached to one end. Also, the sashes served as tumplines, ropes or dog harnesses as needed.*

   Today the Metis have established the "Order of the Sash," which parallels the "Order of Canada," to acknowledge those Metis who have made outstanding contributions to their people and country. Courtesy Glenbow Museum, AP 2213

Chapter Three

Poverty & a Passion for Politics
1920 to 1949

Although most people in Canada enjoyed prosperity in the boom years following the First World War, the lives of many Metis remained isolated and tenuous. They still were itinerant workers, labouring on threshing crews, digging seneca root, cutting and hauling firewood and, in the more northern areas, hunting and trapping. In many ways, their way of life in the 1920s resembled that of Metis at the end of the nineteenth century. Many years later Harriet McCallum, a trapper in northern Saskatchewan and Manitoba, recalled life on the traplines:

we used to paddle all the way to Pelican. It was hard to paddle the river [Churchill], it was rough in some areas because the river was turbulent and strong. We used birch canoes and we had to carry our grub and sleeping gear and anything else we needed. It was hot out and we had to work in the heat because nobody else would do it. While we were on the trip we learned how to provide for ourselves, with the guidance of elders. The portages were extremely hard; the hills were steep, the trail was rugged, the loads were heavy. Our grub box was made out of wood and the contents were heavy. Inside there was dry meat called pemmican, dry sturgeon, bannock, tea, sugar, salt, talopime (this type of grease made very good fry bannock), baking powder, sturgeon oil by the gallon and berries. The trail had to be done, along the way there were bloodthirsty mosquitoes. I went as fast as I could through every portage.

Hundreds of thousands of newcomers continued to settle the West, threatening the future of the Metis, many of whom had achieved little from the scrip program and remained landless and penniless. Of all the numerous questionable dealings by scrip speculators, only one ever reached the attention of Parliament or the public. In 1920 the Metis of Fort Resolution, Fort Smith and Fort Chipewyan presented Prime Minister Arthur Meighen with a petition "asking for a Royal Commission to investigate their grievances in connection with the scrip scandal." Their request was refused, and the government replied that "if there were any frauds perpetrated in connection with [scrip], it was open to them to take the ordinary proceedings before the proper court." Following this advice, some Metis charged Richard Secord, a wealthy businessman in Edmonton, with "the uttering of a forged document in the procuring of the location of land under half-breed scrip." According to the evidence, Secord had bribed a Half-breed woman with ten dollars and a grey shawl to present herself to the scrip commission in 1901 and apply for a certificate on behalf of a resident of Fort Rae. She then received scrip in the Fort Rae individual's name and turned it over to Secord. His son remembers that his father obtained "hundreds of thousands of acres of land," which he then sold for profit to homesteaders.

On 30 May 1921 federal legislation was passed stating that prosecution for an offence concerning Half-breed scrip must be brought within three years of the date of its commission, so the charges against Secord had to be dropped. Because of the timing of this legislation, later generations of Metis raised the question of collusion between the accused and some members of Parliament. The Solicitor General, however, did question the addition of this particular Statute of Limitation to the Criminal Code, and the law was repealed a year later, but the charges against Secord were not raised again.

The attempt to bring this case to court ushered in a new era of political activity by the Metis. In the 1920s, the federal government again took action that would directly affect many Metis without consulting them. Plans were being made to transfer control of Crown lands in the West to the prairie provinces by 1930. Much of this land would then be opened up for settlement, but the Metis had been squatting in some parts of it for several decades. One area directly affected by this move was a settlement near Fishing Lake, Alberta, where a group of Metis had settled at the beginning of the twentieth century. They had no legal right to the land and were unsure of how to approach the government on the issue of making a claim. Finally, in the early 1930s, they came to Joe Dion, an Indian who was the schoolteacher on the nearby Frog Lake Reserve and had sympathy for the Metis. He had often let their children attend his

Pages 92/93: Metis children at Lesser Slave Lake in the 1920s. Courtesy Hugh A. Dempsey

A Metis trapper with his dog and furs in the 1930s. Courtesy Glenbow Museum (Brady Collection), PA 2218-26

school, even though they were not officially entitled to do so.

To the Metis of the Fishing Lake region, the possibility of being evicted from their land at this time was particularly frightening because, like all people in western Canada, they were severely threatened by the Depression. Furthermore, the provincial government not only required them to pay for hunting, trapping and fishing permits but had put restrictions on their freedom to fish throughout the entire year, placing profound hardship on their attempts to earn a living. During this period, the federal government began to enforce strictly the Indian Act's "no trespassing" regulations on Indian reserves, forcing off many Metis who had lived on them for years as integral members of families and communities. Joe Dion recorded the poignant story of a Metis man who lived with the Dion family on the reserve for many years:

an elderly gentleman named Corbett Trottier arrived at our home and asked if he could stay and help around with the chores for his keep . . . we took good care of him and the children soon accepted him as one of the family . . .

One day the Indian agent came around to

Metis trappers at their winter camp in the foothills of the Rockies, Alberta. Courtesy Glenbow Museum (Brady Collection), PA 2218-985

count the cattle, and when he noticed our new tenant he forthwith read him the letter of the law. Corbett had no business on an Indian reserve and he must get out right away. . . . The family was having dinner one day when the agent drove up to the front door. . . . As soon as the agent started on his victim, who by the way was a small man, dad stopped him and, pointing to the old muzzle loader which hung on a rack over the door, he told the agent that the gun was loaded, the cap was on, and it never failed . . .

The agent gazed at dad for a long moment. Finally he said, "All right, Gustave, you win this time. I'll not bother the man as long as he behaves himself."

Mr. Trottier lived as a member of dad's household for over 20 years. This victory on the part of the Indian, however, is an exception; he very seldom had the last word.

Some of the Metis who had gravitated to fringe settlements on the edge of urban centres were also in desperate circumstances. They were unable to obtain relief from any of the communities, as it was given only to those who had paid taxes in better times, and the Metis had always been too poor to do so. But being a resourceful people, they managed to eke out meagre earnings in a variety of ways, some of which were recalled by Mrs. Lena Bellegarde. Her father, Pierre Poitras, worked as a labourer on a large farm at Cupar, Saskatchewan, and her mother, Mary Jean Donaldson, cut and sawed firewood, which she sold in the town of Fort Qu'Appelle. Although the backbreaking work only brought $2.50 a load, it was enough money to feed the family for a week.

Many Metis women worked as domestics, cleaning houses for white people, or as janitors in schools and public buildings. Often an entire family would be working, even the youngest children. Gophers were such pests to western farmers in the 1930s that tails could be sold to municipal officers for one cent each. This provided a limited source of income for many youngsters on the prairies, including Metis children. Coyotes were also bothersome to ranchers and farmers, and the pelts were worth twenty-five to fifty cents each.

As the Depression took its toll and life for the Metis continued into the darkest depths of poverty, many families were broken up by welfare workers. Although extreme poverty may have threatened the physical well-being of some children, their spiritual health was unquestionably devastated by being taken away from families, which were strongly bonded and very close. To avoid the threat of having their children apprehended by welfare officials because there was not enough food in the house, some Metis hunted and trapped illegally in national parks or out of season. The wardens were always watchful for such activity, and no one got away with it for long. Maria Campbell recalls her father being put in handcuffs by the Mountie and disappearing for six months: "He was in jail in Prince Albert.... It was a hard six months for all of us. We had no money and no meat. I had to set rabbit snares every day, and Mom and I would take the .22 and shoot partridges, ducks and whatever we could get. Mom was a terrible hunter." But no matter how destitute Metis families may have been, they always shared what they had. "One thing about our people is that they never hoard. If they have something they share all of it with each other, regardless of good or bad fortune. Maybe that's why we're so damn poor." A major source of protein for many Metis during these hard times was gophers, and Maria Campbell remembers that when they were cooked right, they tasted quite good. First they were skinned, gutted and put "on sticks [which were] pushed into the ground and bent over the fire." The intestines also were "really delicious, roasted and salted."

The Metis were only one of several protest movements that developed during the 1930s in western Canada. Other groups included farmers and workers who were pressuring the government to give them some sort of assistance to ease the problems of the Great Depression.

The desperate situation of the Metis in Alberta finally caught the attention of the provincial government due in part to the political actions of Metis who lived in northern Alberta, one of their last areas of refuge in the early twentieth century. The leaders of this group included men such as Jim Brady, Malcolm Norris, Pete Tomkins and Joe

Dion. All of them, save possibly Pete Tomkins, were somewhat removed ideologically from the people they represented.

Brady, like many Half-breeds, had limited formal education, but was extremely well read. Although most Metis had not spent much time in school as children, some had been nurtured on the works of Shakespeare, Dickens, Sir Walter Scott and Longfellow by their parents who had attended mission schools. Brady's library in his later years rivalled that of any intellectual and reflected his ardent socialism with works by Marx, Engels and Lenin. His home became a centre for discussion on many topics, including politics and Metis history.

Norris, also a socialist, lived in Edmonton for most of his adult life and was well established in the middle class. Joe Dion, a devout Catholic, was a Treaty Indian and had never experienced the "life-in-between" that characterized the existence of many Metis. Pete Tomkins probably knew the plight of his people better than all of them, as he lived in the Metis community of Grouard in northern Alberta. During his political career, Tomkins focussed on obtaining the basic needs of food, clothing and shelter for his people.

In their writings and public statements, it is obvious that Brady and Norris considered themselves as being apart from the people they represented. The fact that they often referred to the Metis as "they" rather than "we" denotes their separation. Norris once declared that "the half-breed is after all but a child, in many instances his mentality is only that of a child." But in 1931 these four men finally brought the Alberta government to action by drawing up a petition that addressed the issue of Metis land tenure; politicians were astounded at the number of people — over 500 — who signed it.

Recognizing that the unrest among these people was serious and that ignoring them would lay the foundation for a larger and more militant political force to mobilize, the provincial government made subtle changes. One of these enabled Metis who had never before been eligible to obtain relief or medical care to receive them in 1934. The church was also aware of the growing movement among the Metis and warned its members to be wary of the "radicals" among them. Under Brady, Norris, Dion and Tomkins, the Metis had become a strong political force, reiterating the demands made by Riel and Dumont in 1885: a land base and an assurance of political autonomy within the federalism of Canada.

The first annual convention of L'Association des Métis d'Alberta et les Territories au Nord-Ouest was held on 28 December 1932. During that meeting, resolutions were passed on the issues of land, registration of trap lines, education and welfare, and were forwarded to the provincial government. Further recognition of Metis grievances came in 1935 with the appointment of the Half-Breed Commission, later known as the Ewing Commission (after the judge who headed it), "to inquire into the conditions of the Metis, with reference to health, education and welfare, and to make recommendations to rectify the situation." J. M. Dechene, a member of the Alberta legislature, made an unsuccess-

ful attempt to have a Metis appointed to the commission.

One of the first questions the Ewing Commission had to deal with was to define exactly who was a Half-breed or a Metis. After lengthy discussion over the amount of Indian blood that a Metis ought to have, they agreed it was impossible to establish an arithmetical blood formula to determine a person's right to claim status as a Metis or Half-breed. Norris maintained that "if he has a drop of Indian blood in his veins and has not been assimilated in the social fabric of our civilization [he] is a Metis." Eventually, the commission decided that to be a Metis, a person had to either look like an Indian or be able to establish Indian ancestry. Another important component of the definition was that the person had to live "the life of an ordinary Indian," the exact details of which were not given. It was further agreed that Non-treaty Indians would be included. Thus, the commission averted its attention from "respectable Metis," defined as those who had settled down to farm life or were integrated into the society at large and, instead, decided to focus on the nomadic Metis and Indians who had refused treaty and taken scrip and were the most destitute of the Native population.

The commission heard testimony from the clergy, doctors, MLAs and representatives of the Metis Association. A. F. Ewing, as chairman, would not allow discussion to dwell on the issue of scrip, nor would he allow the four men who represented the Metis to discuss how their people had been denied access to land. During the hearings, it was clear that one policy would not satisfy all the

Members of the Metis Association of Alberta, with some of those who testified before the Ewing Commission, 1935. Back row, L–R: Joseph Dechene, MLA; Felix Calihoo; Leonidas Giroux, MLA; Peter Tomkins, Jr. Front row, L–R: Jim Brady; Rev. Father Falher; Joe Dion; Rev. Bishop Guy; Malcolm Norris; Peter Tomkins, Sr. Courtesy Glenbow Museum, NA 1899-8

Oman, a Half-breed Cree, at Churchill, Manitoba, 1926. Photograph by L. T. Burwash, courtesy Public Archives of Canada (Indian and Northern Affairs Collection), PA-99526

groups who testified, because in many ways their views were in direct opposition to each other. Even among the four representatives of the Metis Association there were differing opinions. Dion felt the answer was for the Metis to be assimilated, with some attention to a recognition of their cultural heritage, and in previous years he had organized a dance troupe towards this end. Norris and Brady saw the Metis problem as a class struggle and wanted land "for the purpose of permitting them to develop their own form of economy and to structure their relations with the greater society in their own way."

On the other hand, the clergy were in favour of federal control of the Metis and wanted the church to be responsible for their education. Norris and Brady were adamantly opposed to this because the Metis Association had been founded as a nonreligious organization. The church also advocated that children should receive an "elementary" education, including the basics of reading, writing and arithmetic, and that boys learn the essentials of ranching and farming, "while the girls should be taught the elements of sanitation, cleanliness, sewing and knitting." Still, some clergy thought that no matter what efforts at education were made, the Metis would "remain a good, big child with the qualities and deficiencies of the age."

Frightening health statistics were brought forward during the hearings, indicating that ninety per cent of the Metis had tuberculosis and that fifty to sixty per cent suffered some form of communicable disease. In the end the commission felt that this was an exaggeration, and one doctor testified that these statistics were no different from those once found among the population of Alberta as a whole.

To improve the health, education and welfare of the Metis, the commission recommended that they be given allotments of land with agricultural potential and timber resources, distant from white settlement and adjacent to land available for expansion. By moving the Metis to concentrated settlements, medical clinics could be set up and schools built, and people could establish an agricultural base while continuing to hunt and trap. Since many Metis problems were attributed to their failure to adapt to white ways, as well as their inability to handle money, this proposal suggested keeping them separate from white society. The commission did not want to upset the "general public" in any way in reaching a solution.

The Metis leaders wanted to have the colonies run by Metis Association delegates representing the local councils, with any staff responsible to the local councils. The clergy recommended the formation of a general council on which there would be church representation. In the end, the Alberta government decided to run the colonies through a supervisor who would be responsible to a government agency, with a Metis council that would function in an advisory capacity only.

On the colonies, the emphasis was to be agriculture, and after a settler was accepted, he had to meet the standard regulations of homesteading: establish residence on his parcel of land within thirty days, build a house within ninety days and a shelter for livestock within a year. He was also required to cultivate a

Pages 102/103: Half-breed children dressed for school at Fort Chipewyan, Alberta, 1931. Courtesy Public Archives of Canada, PA-14406

This page: An Indian and Metis pilgrimage to the Catholic shrine near Duck Lake, Saskatchewan, 1928. Courtesy Glenbow Museum, NA 871-1

garden to meet the needs of his family and clear two acres (0.8 ha) of land per year up to a minimum of fifteen acres (6 ha). In addition to colonies, the commission recommended that 320 acres (130 ha) be allotted to individuals in areas where they would be able to make a living from hunting and trapping. They were to receive free hunting and fishing permits and have preference over others in respect to fur, game and fish resources.

Although the recommendations of the commission did not support the way that the Metis wanted the colonies to be governed, they did offer to some of the people a hope for the future. The conclusions of the commission were incorporated into the Metis Betterment Act, passed by the Alberta legislature on 22 November 1938.

In spite of efforts to organize the Metis, many were still averse to any communal effort and did not join the organizations. In January 1939 Norris tried to organize an Interlakes Fish Pool at Wabamun, Alberta, an area with a large Metis population. The co-operative was a failure, because the Metis, "revealing their traditional individualism, sold [their fish] to private companies whenever they offered higher prices than the co-ops."

Joe Dion also lamented the problems of trying to organize the independent Metis. Despite the efforts of dedicated men, "the lack of cooperation on the part of those [the Metis] they were trying to help," plus their own lack of understanding of Metis ways and attitudes, led to failure.

In Alberta the colonies continued to take shape amidst much criticism, and by 1941 there were nearly three hundred families living on them. Despite this, the Metis Association of Alberta, which had worked so hard to obtain some form of land base for its members, was beginning to lose its strength, and had essentially disappeared by 1942. Brady, one of the men so instrumental in its creation, reflected that "the association was created by the economic forces which created havoc with us during the depression and there was a crying need for it. With a change to better times . . . that need was negated to some extent."

The Metis of Alberta were not the only ones in western Canada who managed to bring attention to their plight. In the mid-1930s Joseph Ross, a Metis labourer from Regina, felt that his people needed an organization to pressure the Saskatchewan government to help get them jobs, relief and education, as well as to recognize their claims for land. He organized a meeting of seventeen individuals who called themselves the "true halfbreeds of Saskatchewan": this was the beginning of the Saskatchewan Metis Society. Although centred in Regina, the society attempted to organize locals throughout the province. Membership was restricted to Metis and did not include Nontreaty Indians.

As with all fledgling organizations, funds were very short. Because Joe Ross was blind, he could travel free on the train, and this helped to save money during the efforts to organize the rest of the province. For many people, involvement in the society resulted in introductions to Metis communities and families they had not known existed before.

Although in this early stage the Metis Society was trying to bring people together, it ran into problems that are still evident today. The Metis in the north lived a lifestyle very similar to that of their Cree relatives, hunting and trapping and still speaking only Cree. Those in the south spoke mainly English with some French and relied heavily on the white community for jobs or relief. In the north the Metis wanted a land base; in the south they wanted vocational training to enable them to integrate into the labour force.

The Saskatchewan Metis Society received a grant from the provincial government in 1940 to hire the legal firm of Noonan and Hodges to study their land claims. The province had offered them land in 1939, but they had turned it down in lieu of receiving money to pay for legal advice in their fight with the federal government for a land settlement. The study, funded by the meagre funds of the Saskatchewan Metis Society, was not released until 1943. While the report acknowledged the Metis con-

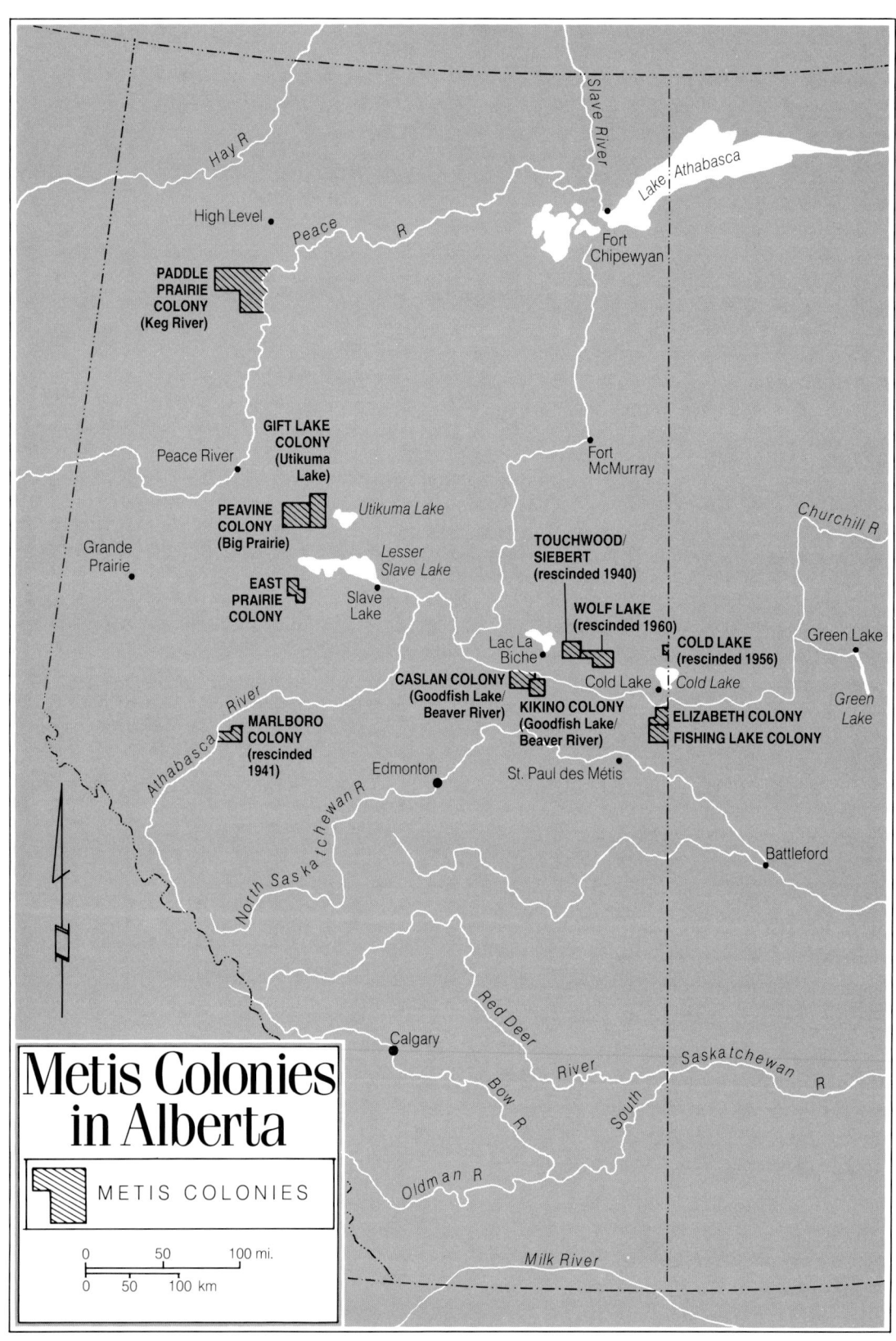

tribution in earlier eras as scouts, guides and "peacemakers, negotiators and liaison officers between the whites and Indians," it concluded that the Metis might have a moral claim against the federal government to demand a settlement, but any legal claim had been eradicated by the issue of scrip. The report recommended they seek compensation or welfare for their current situation and went on to say the Metis would have rejected any scheme designed to "train and fit them for civilization," implying that the Metis of the nineteenth century had received what they had wanted under the scrip program.

By 1949, with improving economic conditions on the prairies, the organizations formed to help alleviate poverty among the Metis, including the Saskatchewan Metis Society, essentially died.

Governments in both Manitoba and Saskatchewan attempted to implement programs to help the situation of Metis hunters and trappers in the north in the mid-1940s. Their livelihood was being seriously threatened by two events: the development of artificial furs, which were much cheaper than real furs, and the population growth in the north, which resulted in overtrapping in some areas. In 1945 the socialist-oriented Saskatchewan government established the Fur Marketing Board and the block conservation system to help remedy this situation. The marketing board was a nonprofit Crown corporation designed to break the monopoly of the major fur buyers, including the Hudson's Bay Company. Trappers sold their furs directly to the board and received payment in two installments, the first immediately and the second after the fur was sold at market. Although this system was meant to help trappers by removing the middleman, it ended up making them worse off than ever because it altered their traditional way of doing business and the basis of their social structure. For generations they had been able to obtain credit for supplies to last them the entire trapping season; the better at hunting that a man was, the more credit he could receive, and the greater his community prestige. But now that the Hudson's Bay Company and other private traders were not guaranteed payment in furs, they often refused to give anything but small amounts of credit. Thus, trappers could go out on their lines for only short periods of time. Furthermore, often they could ill afford to wait for their second payment, and when it arrived, their debts at the store often consumed it, leaving nothing with which to buy supplies for the next season. Because the cheques usually arrived by mail, small settlements of transients developed around post offices, as trappers awaited the arrival of their money.

The block conservation system was an effort to restore the beaver and muskrat resources in the north by assigning specific areas to individual trappers, with a small central settlement being created to serve several trapping areas. In this centre, it was hoped that schools could be developed and that trappers would plant small vegetable gardens to provide them with food through the winter. Unfortunately, Metis houses lacked

107

Previous page: A Metis family, the Trottiers, at Fishing Lake, Saskatchewan, 1936. Courtesy Glenbow Museum (Brady Collection), PA 2218-122

facilities for storing vegetables; also, most northern Metis trappers were not accustomed to eating vegetables. In response to this program one novice farmer, who was not "content to grow just vegetables, planted peanuts, tobacco and Solon berries." Although he never harvested a crop from any of them, he was "very proud to have been the first Metis in the north to grow them." Eventually, the block conservation system resulted in many families living in the settlements and receiving welfare. With more time on their hands, alcohol became a greater problem, leading to an increase in crime and violence in the northern communities.

Another program implemented by the Saskatchewan government was an attempt to establish an agricultural community at Green Lake, which had been a pemmican station on the fur trade routes and therefore had a long history of Metis settlement. Prior to 1940 Metis in the area had been scattered in the forest, living in small sod huts and surviving on rations of flour, sugar and tea bought with "relief" money, supplemented by some fish and small animals, which they hunted. Local Metis, as well as those from the south, were enticed to move to Green Lake by the promise of land and employment.

Henry Pelletier, who was living at Lestock in southern Saskatchewan, was encouraged by government officials to go, and against the wishes of his wife, they left their home and headed north. On leaving Lestock, their home was burned (he assumed by municipal officials), so they could not return if they did not find their new location satisfactory. When they arrived at Green Lake, "they realized that there was nothing there for them." Of the instructor who was there to teach them to be farmers, Mr. Pelletier commented, "I forgot more about farming than he ever knew." Those who came from the south were horrified at the living conditions of the Metis at Green lake: "They had only tables of logs, home made stools; none of them had chairs and tables like we did. . . . We were kings compared to them." Life in the north was also most uncomfortable for the newcomers: "the blackflies drove us crazy, my face was swollen up and the horses were all bleeding. The mosquitoes were so big you could use them as milk stools." The family returned to Lestock, where Pelletier managed to find work hauling firewood with his horses, but he was forced to take relief in the winter.

Green Lake was described as a great success by some who claimed that the "unutterable filth of a decade ago has been replaced in most instances by something approaching cleanliness" and "after a while the Metis gradually became accustomed to the idea that work [wasn't] as bad as they might once have thought." The settlement did not actually meet with much success, however, since the government did not give settlers the support and the resources necessary for them to become farmers. Although the intention of the government to improve the lot of the Metis had been good in principle, most of the programs appeared to have been organized without consulting the Metis themselves to determine what the real problems were and therefore most often failed.

In the 1930s and 1940s, despite destitution, and amid valiant struggles to unify the Metis politically, the flamboyant aspects of their social life continued. Boisterous, fun-filled dances were often held, such as the one Maria Campbell recalled:

After supper, furniture was moved out against the wall or put outside while the fiddlers tuned their fiddles. Soon they were sawing out a mean hoedown or a Red River jig, and everyone was dancing. Everybody was enjoying themselves, dancing and eating, when suddenly a fight broke out. . . . The mothers chased all the little kids under the beds and we big ones climbed up to the beams to watch. Soon everyone was fighting and no one knew who was hitting who . . . we never had a dance without a good fight and we enjoyed and looked forward to it as much as we did to the dancing.

No matter how little money the Metis had, someone in the community always found enough to buy a fiddle. Mrs. Lena Bellegarde recalled that in the 1930s people no longer made their own instruments. At dances or just for family entertainment her father played the fiddle and her uncle played the mouth organ. Like many Metis musicians, Mrs. Bellegarde's father had learned to play from his father.

When dances were held in the Fort Qu'Appelle region, everyone came, and after the dance ended, a collection was taken to pay the fiddler. At some point in every dance, the group would proudly sing some of the songs that told of the heritage of the Metis people. This tradition reached back to the days of the voyageurs, when many hours were passed in the canoe or around the campfire singing of their lives. Many of the songs had been passed down from one generation to the next. Pierre Falcon, the bard of the Metis nation, had been the first to write down the songs of the Half-breeds following the Battle of Seven Oaks.

Tragically, once poverty became entrenched as a way of life for Metis, many of the distinguishable elements of their lives, including their individual style of dress, became less readily obvious. Many wore only cast-off clothing given to them as charity by local white residents, but often the older generations persevered in their traditions. Maria Campbell remembers Cheechum, her grandmother, wearing "black, ankle-length skirts and black blouses with full sleeves and high collars. Around her neck were four or five strings of beads and a chain made of copper wire. On her wrists were copper bracelets which she wore to ward off arthritis. She wore moccasins and tight leggings — these were covered with a bright porcupine quill design." In the past, Metis women had been known to wear black frequently, and most Metis had worn brightly coloured moccasins.

Their homes resembled those of earlier times, as did the furnishings. Often beds and chairs were made from roughly hewn pieces of wood or small branches, with rawhide lacings to form the seat of a chair or base for a mattress. Frequently, a bed served as a chesterfield during the day, due to the limited amount of space and furniture available. In some houses, however, there was in "the living-room area . . . a homemade chesterfield and chair of carved wood and woven rawhide, a couple of rocking chairs painted red, and an old steamer trunk."

Maria Campbell recalled from her childhood that "there was a large table, two chairs and two benches made from wide planks, which we scrubbed with homemade lye soap after each meal. . . . The floor was made of wide planks which were scoured to an even whiteness all over."

Poles were often placed across the ceiling, and furs were hung to dry there for the winter. On the wall hung pots, pans and various roots and herbs used for cooking and making medicine. Maria Campbell wrote: "On a cold winter night the smell of moose stew simmering on the stove blended with the wild smell of drying skins of mink, weasels and squirrels, and the spicy herbs and roots hanging from the walls."

Young Metis girls were still taught to

Discing on a Metis community farm at Keg River, Saskatchewan, 1942. Courtesy Glenbow Museum (Brady Collection), PA 2218-202

weave red willow bark baskets, which were used for berry picking, laundry or storage. Braided rugs were scattered on the floor, and many long winter nights were spent making them. Some of these rugs were made for sale and were in the same colourful tradition as much of their beadwork and embroidery.

Mission schools still influenced the embroidery and needlework done by Metis women, particularly in the north. Sister Leduc, a member of the Order of the Grey Nuns, worked in various northern communities for nearly thirty years, teaching needlework to young girls. Initially, she would design patterns for them to follow or use commercial patterns and would make them redo a piece several times until it was done satisfactorily. Many of her students proved to be

A Metis survey party taking a meal break in the Keg River area of Saskatchewan, 1942. Courtesy Glenbow Museum (Brady Collection), PA 2218-206

skilled in their craft, and she would let them design their own patterns, which were heavily influenced by the instruction they had received, yet undoubtedly incorporated elements of their own traditions and personal expression. The items of clothing or household decorations that a few Metis women continued to make for sale or for their own use provided them with a treasured element of colour and gaiety in those desperate times.

At the beginning of the Depression, many of the Metis were at the bottom rung of the economic scale and their existence became even more precarious as the hard times continued. Their subsistence sank to depths difficult to imagine. It is ironic that it took a war to bring economic relief to them as well as to many other Canadians. In common with many other residents of the prairies, the Metis were eager to join the armed forces at the beginning of the 1940s to relieve the poverty that haunted them daily. According to some sources, the highest per capita voluntary enlistment for the Second World War in Canada was amongst the Native peoples, who enlisted in many different regiments in all parts of the country. The anonymity of many of the Metis who enlisted in this war was the same as that of the First World War; thus, the exact number of those who enlisted is unknown.

Metis leaders including Malcolm Norris and Jim Brady also joined up, the former in the army and later the RCAF, the latter in the Royal Canadian Artillery. They considered the growth of the Nazi movement in Europe to be more

115

Mrs. Gerald Webster (née Belcourt), a granddaughter of Simon Fraser and Sophie Brazeau, in the 1920s. Photograph by Courtlands Gallery, courtesy Glenbow Museum, NA 2365-108

threatening than their own problems, as Brady explained to the Metis Association convention in 1942: "our true destiny is not bound by the success or failure attendant upon Metis deliberation. . . . It is bound up with our continued existence as Canadians who fight [for] those liberties to which we are all devoted and the preservation of which is dependant upon our victory."

Canadian involvement in the war had many different ramifications for those who stayed at home. Spurred by the war effort, Indian farmers increased their production to levels they had not achieved before, and the Metis, too, were much more productive. Northern Saskatchewan, where commercial fishing had been practised for many years, became "Canada's leading producer of whitefish and was supplying almost one-third of the trout." This increase in the fishing improved the condition of residents in the area, many of whom were Metis. Those who remained at home were also affected by such events as the construction of the Alaska Highway. Although northern Alberta had been a thoroughfare to the north ever since the days of the Klondike Gold Rush in the late 1890s, the mass movement of over 200 000 American troops and equipment through the isolated region reinforced to many Metis the realities of the twentieth century.

But most significantly, when the men who participated in the war came home, they had a new orientation to the world. For an intellectual like Brady, observations made during his time in France reinforced his belief in the intellectual heritage of some of his Metis brothers. After engaging "in a pleasant conversational contre-temps with two attractive Belgian ladies on subjects both divine and profane," Brady recorded in his diary that "their intellectual attitudes were a forceful example of the truism that only French culture had pointed the way to the art of truly civilized living." For although not of French ancestry himself, he had grown up in St. Paul, surrounded by French-Canadian settlers from Quebec and French Metis. His first

Pete and Justine Cardinal at Islay, Alberta, circa 1940. Pete Cardinal helped to guard prisoners of war in Alberta. Courtesy Glenbow Museum, NA 3686-26

Private J. G. Poitras (left) and Private E. J. Poitras (right), after enlistment in the South Saskatchewan Regiment, 1941. Courtesy Glenbow Museum, NA 4712-2

exposure to the roots of their heritage strongly affected him.

For other Metis, overseas duty had a more practical result. Their common experience of the war in Europe bonded many of the veterans together, and their military training and experiences led to more satisfying and better-paid jobs such as Department of Natural Resources patrolmen, RCMP special constables and telegraph operators. Some stayed in the forces to become career military men, while others started businesses such as pool rooms, trading stores and contract companies. In fact, very few veterans returned to a life based on fishing and trapping.

The war involvement of some Metis rekindled in them the fire to begin again the struggle for their rights, particularly in places such as Cumberland House in northern Saskatchewan, where there was potential for them to become self-sufficient. Although in 1950 they were still leading a mobile life, hunting and trapping and returning to the community seasonally, not one member of that community was receiving welfare. The Department of Natural Resources attempted to set up an experimental farm to attract the Metis to a more sedentary life, which would facilitate better health care and education as the children would have access year-round to schools. Eventually, the farm was declared a failure, again because the farming practices and background of the management failed to take into account the way of life and culture of the people. Within their established lifestyle, the Metis flourished, but any attempt to impose a change on that lifestyle without consulting them was bound to fail.

In the immediate postwar era, Canada's north began to open for development, and multinational companies began exploration for resources. Initially, they saw the Native population as an available employment base, and the government hoped that this activity would lead to the integration of the Metis into mainstream society. Unfortunately, employers had no understanding of the cultural gap that separated them from their Metis employees, who placed priority on obligations to family and kinship groups over employers and who were not used to the white business world's structured work habits and deadlines. Racial discrimination began to emerge, and soon any development that did begin in the north was usually staffed with whites from the south, who were paid high wages to come and live in the hinterland.

As the urban population of Metis and Indians continued to grow through the 1940s and 1950s, the old problems of discrimination and poverty still festered; the need for new solutions would see the Metis mobilize themselves again into political organizations.

Chapter Four

Rekindling the Fires
1950 to 1969

Pages 120/121: Horses were still a common form of transportation in many Metis communities in the 1950s. Photograph by Mike Kesterton for the Canadian Geographic Society

In Canada the 1950s were characterized by the Korean War, a heady economic boom and a growth in consciousness of social problems. During the war, the federal government encouraged enlistment in the armed forces, and a number of Metis joined up, as they had in the two world wars and for much the same reasons — to escape poverty. At home, the majority of Metis did not share in the nation's general prosperity, but governments did instigate a proliferation of anthropological and sociological studies on the Metis, well aware that they knew very little about these descendants of the fur traders and their Native wives; they also knew that their programs to ease Metis poverty had met with limited success.

The first major study was done under the direction of Jean Lagasse of the Social and Economic Research office of Manitoba. Legislation passed in 1956 directed Lagasse to investigate the "living conditions of the Indians and Metis . . . with a view to discovering whether their social integration and economic advancement could be facilitated." During the debate over the bill, legislators expressed "a considerable degree of anxiety . . . about the future hardships which this population would face if help was not received immediately." The debate reflected not only a sense of pride in these citizens who had contributed to the development of the West, but also a feeling of "regret, perhaps guilt, because this population was now scattered in the most unproductive areas of the province, existing at best, in a condition of independence created by physical and cultural isolation and at worst, in idleness, hunger and disease." It was hoped that with an adequate program of assistance, these people could still "recapture the spirit of initiative and courage" that had characterized them in the past.

When the study began, researchers assumed that about 10 000 people of Indian ancestry were living in the province, a figure based on a 1941 census that had counted 8962 Metis. Eventually, the study grew to include 23 579 Metis as well as 2373 Indians living off reserves. One of the biggest problems Lagasse had was identifying the Metis population. Many of those who qualified denied being Metis because they had been taught to be ashamed of their heritage, and as a result, identification was sometimes made by another individual: "he is a half-breed alright, but don't tell him I said so because he does not like to be called that." Initially, the study group thought they might be able to identify Metis by examining the voting lists, but "a municipal official confessed that names of Metis families likely to become indigent had not been included on a Provincial list 'for fear they believe they have earned residence in our town and request financial assistance.'" Although eighty per cent of those in Manitoba who could call themselves Metis were not readily identifiable, some still participated in the social and cultural aspects of their heritage. At the 1958 meeting of L'Union Nationale Métisse St. Joseph du Manitoba, originally formed in 1887 as a social and cultural society, there were four hundred to five hundred Metis in attendance, none of whom was included in the Lagasse study because they had integrated into the larger society.

Lagasse used criteria such as "language, physical appearance, surname,

Victor Poitras from Lebret, Saskatchewan, serving in Korea. Like many other Metis, he stayed in the service after World War II to make it his career. Courtesy Glenbow Museum PA 2639-1

Facing page: A Metis man setting his traps in northern Saskatchewan. In the postwar era, as it is today, trapping continued to be a viable lifestyle for some Metis. Photograph by Mike Kesterton for the Canadian Geographic Society

background of usual associates or friends, behaviour, and level of occupation" to identify Metis. The study found that often they could be identified by their poverty.

In 1959 Lagasse and his researchers completed their study and recommended that the Metis should be consulted and have an active role in the creation of government programs, a desire that harked back to Metis sentiments of nearly a hundred years before. It further recommended that legislation be passed to fight the prejudice they found was rampant in the province of Manitoba. The Lagasse study pointed out the need for similar investigations in other provinces, because the Metis situation was complex and required localized analysis. Metis problems were not amenable to simple solutions.

Across the prairies Metis frequently lived on the edge of white communities in fringe settlements that had been given names such as Rooster Town, Smokey Hollow, Bannock Town and Fort Tuyau (the French term for pipe). These settlements provided the Metis with a window on the white world, which more than anything heightened their sense of isolation and frustration: they knew they would never be allowed access to it unless they could hide their ancestry in some way. Thus, they ended up "mid way between two worlds." Many of them held semiskilled, seasonal jobs, including digging seneca root, picking berries, collecting frogs (for their legs) and harvesting wild rice, and were always ready to move on. Some ran small stores or businesses that served mainly their own settlements. Very few of them participated in any form of farming, because even in the 1950s they were forced to practise undercapitalized agriculture, though some had small gardens producing vegetables such as potatoes, which formed an integral part of their diet.

Metis who lived on the edge of Indian reserves followed an Indian way of life. Many of the men were married to Indian women, who consequently had lost their Indian status and their right to live on reserves.

Fringe settlements on the edge of towns had few or no services, as the residents paid no taxes; nor did settlements near reserves, as the federal government, which serviced the reserves, drew the line sharply on the boundaries. Generally, the educational level of Metis was not high, with very few attending school past grade five or six. There were several reasons for this, including the fact that young people had to work to help support their families. Often they were only allowed access to schools through the generosity of a nearby reserve, but if the school became crowded, the Metis were asked to leave. Moreover, their transient lifestyle often dictated that children stay in school for only part of the year. Finally, many students lost interest in an education that often had very little relevance to their daily lives.

Metis settlements varied little from those described many decades earlier, except that their cabins were in sharp contrast to the modern plywood houses built for government officials, police and medical workers. A typical northern community consisted of "rough log cabins surrounding a mission and one or

Green Lake school in the early 1950s. The church continued to play a very important role in the formal education of many Metis. Photograph by Mike Kesterton for the Canadian Geographic Society

more trading posts," often built on a transportation route such as a river or a lake.

In many ways Metis homes were similar to those of Indians in the north. They usually consisted of one room with little furniture, including a wooden bedstead, a small tin stove, a wooden table and a limited number of cooking and eating utensils. "The walls are too bare, but may often be decorated with calendars, religious pictures, personal photographs. ... It still appeared that the entire house's contents could be packed at a moment's notice and transported by toboggan or canoe." Generally, the houses were neat and clean, as "untidiness is a subject for ridicule." Because there were not enough beds for everyone in the family as well as for those who stayed with the family for an evening or for several months, many slept on the floor. But each day they packed away the bedding, cleared the floor of debris and stored items for cooking and eating in the grub box.

Although Lagasse noted that one way to identify a Metis house was that it usually would not be modern, perhaps only a cardboard-and-tarpaper shack, many Metis do live like other members of the Canadian community. For example, along the Saskatchewan River at Batoche today, their homes look like those of any other farming family in the area; some differ only in that they are less ornate and have fewer examples of folk art adorning their fences and buildings. Apart from a few examples of "gorgeous sky blue," the Metis seem to have decorated their homes modestly on the exterior, if at all.

Metis who gravitated to the cities usu-

A Metis man and his grandchild. Family unity is integral to the lifestyle of many Metis. Photograph by Mike Kesterton for the Canadian Geographic Society

Metis women from Green Lake, Saskatchewan, decorating moccasins with beadwork. Most of these items were made for sale. Photograph by Mike Kesterton for the Canadian Geographic Society

ally ended up living in the poor sections, since if they could get any jobs at all, they were the lowest-paying ones. The urban situation was frightening and unfamiliar to many Metis. In the city they were often far from family and friends who, if they could not provide financial help, did at least lend moral support and create a sense of community spirit. Traditions from the past, such as card games and lively dances, sustained that spirit and continue to do so today.

In card games, players use traps, rifle shells, matches, fishing nets or other personal equipment for bets when money is scarce. Both men and women are always keen to join a card game and gamble, but never to the point of destitution. In Metis villages today, local bingos are also very popular and are major social events.

At Green Lake, Saskatchewan, in the 1950s nearly every member of the community could play the fiddle, guitar or banjo, and traditional dances such as the Red River jig, schottische and the two-step were still popular. Small dance parties still occurred spontaneously in someone's cabin, with all the furniture moved out for the event. At one dance held in Lebret, Saskatchewan, in 1957, the best dancer in the area was asked to perform for a group of visitors. He was in "fine form" and duly impressed the guests, but suddenly, in the middle of his performance, he fled from the room in a panic and was not seen for several hours. When he returned, he shamefacedly admitted that during his performance he had had a mental block and could remember only twenty-one of the thirty-three jigging steps he knew.

Other Metis traditions are also widely followed, especially that of bringing in the New Year. In some communities, it is the major event of the winter season, perhaps because its origins lie in both the Scottish and French heritage of the Metis. An elderly Metis recounted the custom of "kissing in the New Year," a tradition stretching back at least three generations in his family: "My father continued to follow the custom handed to him by his dad. It was a custom within Metis families from long ago to the turn of the century to request from the priest, the New Year's blessing. My Grandfather, as head of the family would go forth and obtain it. Upon receiving it, he would then come home and there, starting with his wife and then the children from the eldest to the youngest, he would, in turn, bless them. Then the New Year's kissing would start."

On New Year's Day, families celebrate by moving from house to house, the group gradually getting larger and larger. Each household provides a warm welcome and refreshments, as people sing, dance and entertain each other. All of them eventually stop at one house and remain there to dance, in true Metis fashion, far into the night. This tradition led to talent contests becoming an integral part of some Metis gatherings and includes talent of every kind: contemporary musicians who model themselves on rock stars to good old country-and-western bands, with spoon players and fiddlers, as well as choral groups. At the conclusion of the event, the audience selects the winners. To entertain one another is not enough; an extra spark is added to the evening by making it competitive.

Jigging and fiddling contests are also common, and participation is the main factor, with everyone taking part in the initial stages — even those who have never danced a step of a Red River jig before.

In Alberta in the early 1950s, surveys of the Metis on the colonies and those resident in other areas of northern Alberta showed an alarming number of cases of tuberculosis. Again, this pointed out the need to have more information about the numbers and life conditions of the Metis in the province. Under the auspices of the Alberta Tuberculosis Association, Dr. B. Y. Card was asked to do a study to bring to light knowledge "that might find application in constructive programmes for raising the level of living and health of the Metis." The study concluded that the factors that had lead to a high incidence of tuberculosis in the 1930s had not really changed. As one man explained:

I know what started it really. It was when I had pneumonia . . . I didn't have the proper treatment. I had the flu and had to go out in a chinook. One of my kids . . . was dying and I went at night to get some stuff in the

Prime Minister John Diefenbaker and Saskatchewan Metis leaders. The political battles of the Metis and Native people in general were acknowledged as issues for serious consideration during the Diefenbaker era. Courtesy Aboriginal Multi-Media Society of Alberta

store. . . . At night I couldn't see. I slipped on the road. It was pretty wet. I was pretty feverish. And I didn't get no treatment. And it happened that very same day or day before my little house got burned. . . . There was chinook winds. There was water all over. The next day was cold, cold blizzard. . . . There was no gravel roads then. They [whites] tried it with cars but I couldn't make it [to High Prairie and the nearest doctor]. Finally we did make it, but it was about 10 to 15 days after when I catch this pneumonia. . . . So doctor give me examination. He told me, "You're very sick. You shouldn't be up. You go back home and stay in bed and don't never get up 'till you're well." So I did. [Then] I went to hospital. I stayed two months. The air get my lungs, just burned me. Cold air. The child die. I didn't even go to the funeral. All that summer and spring I was very sick. But I had to . . . do some kind of work to eat.

The problems of poor housing, distance from hospital services, dependence on the white population for help, lack of personal transportation and the constant struggle to make a living all contributed to the poor health of these people. As in Manitoba, the Metis of Alberta were found to be in a worse situation than many Indians. The Card study concluded that Metis problems could no longer be looked upon as something unique to their people but were similar to those of the poor in any place in Canada. Their situation was aggravated, however, by the racial prejudice to which they were subjected.

By the mid-1950s welfare formed approximately one-half of the income of some Metis families, who faced increased deterioration in health, alcohol-related problems and a continually decreasing self-image. The Welfare Council of Greater Winnipeg, which dealt with Metis in this tragic situation, began in 1955 to hold annual conferences of Indians and Metis to "discuss the issues facing native people." Native populations were seen as a singular entity, and not until some years later did the differences between Metis and Indians surface clearly. But in the 1950s many of their problems were the same — destitution, sickness and a dismal perspective on the future — creating unity between them, even if at times it was only a political front to emphasize their common plight.

In the north, poverty continued to worsen in the 1960s, as only about twenty per cent of the population in any settlement had work, and few trappers had the necessary cash to buy winter supplies. Furthermore, due to declining fur resources and a decrease in demand, it was impossible to make a living from hunting and trapping. Fortunately, the northern Metis still possessed a strong kinship network, which bonded them together and aided those in dire need.

Although tourism had become well developed in the north, it did not provide the jobs for the Native population that the government had hoped it would. Much of the money from the tourists found its way only into the pockets of the white population, which owned the stores, cafes and guiding businesses servicing the tourists. Although some Metis and Indians were employed as guides, bad weather, poor fishing and cancelled reservations cut considerably into their income; a few who became regular employees of certain tourist camps did better. Increasing development in the north led to the need for improved transportation systems and gave some northerners work on summer road crews. Fish-packing plants and mink farms also provided some employment, but poverty continued to be a serious problem.

In September 1964 the newly elected Liberal premier of Saskatchewan, Ross Thatcher, called a conference of all Indian and Metis leaders in the province to confirm his campaign commitment to help the Native people. However, his efforts backfired. Metis leader Malcolm Norris attended the conference and not only derided the failure of many government programs to help his people but accused his Indian brothers of hiding on their reserves in fear of the white man. Division among the Metis was also apparent: twenty-five northern communities sent representatives to the conference, but only three from the south did so. Although language and lifestyle continued to divide them as they had done twenty years earlier, the real division was political. Northern Metis wanted to work against the government; those from the south wished to work with the government. Finally, in 1966, the Metis Association of Saskatchewan was formed, though response to join was not immediate. Norris and others worked hard to bolster the strength of the organization, emphasizing that the Metis had to improve their self-respect while understanding the "need for unity in the struggle for self-determination."

In 1966 the Alberta government authorized a study of the Metis in the northeastern part of the province who were labelled as a poverty group. Anthropologists who lived on the Metis colonies and others who researched the Metis living in surrounding settlements found that housing was insufficient, often not adequate to keep out the ravages of a northern winter. People commonly lived in one- or two-room log cabins insulated with mud, with neither electricity nor plumbing. The drinking water was polluted, leading to such intestinal problems that many considered diarrhea a normal state. Venereal disease, tuberculosis and measles were also rampant. Their diet was lacking in nutritional value, and a standard meal often included only bannock, lard, potatoes and tea, with meat served only about once a day, six days a week. Sometimes their diet was supplemented by gardening and fishing. Isolation still posed problems in terms of access to health care and employment opportunities.

On occasion the Metis took great exception to the blanket image of them that these studies presented. Mrs. Dorothy Miller of Amisk, Alberta, pointed out:

It is the white peoples' prejudice that makes some Metis people unsure of themselves . . . [but] I and many of my friends here do not live that way, we feel we are just as good as whites or anybody else. We are fishermen. You do not see only bread, tea and lard on our breakfast table; our children have a choice of eggs, cereal and anything they want for breakfast. We have meat on the table for lunch and dinner. We have an abundance of vegetables because we grow our own. . . . Our children go to school well dressed and well fed. The reason some drop out of school is because the whites turn their noses up and call them names over their nationality. Our homes are not one-room shacks, but large enough for our families, with bedrooms and good beds in them. Some families around here have TV. Most of the families have good books. I, myself have the best encyclopedia that you can buy, and believe me, it is well used.

As Dorothy Miller's comments suggest, many writers have focussed on the lower levels of Metis society, ignoring the accomplishments and achievements of a large part of the population.

Researchers in the 1966 Alberta study began to realize that the Metis were not as hopeless and demoralized as they had been described; rather, they were "frustrated and disgusted" with being treated like children by governments and being discriminated against by the general population. Moreover, they insisted on retaining their culture and heritage instead of becoming "white" as many government programs encouraged.

This atmosphere renewed their desire to organize and voice their discontent to the government. The Metis Association of Alberta, first formed in the 1930s, was rejuvenated in the 1960s under the direction of leaders such as Stan Daniels and Adrian Hope. The association turned its attention immediately to the subject of land claims research. From 1967 to 1972 the association grew from 50 members to 3000, and the funds it managed increased from $3,000 to $1,000,000. Recruitment of members was not always easy, because of the reluctance among Metis to join organizations or to accept one authority. Harold Desjarlais, a field worker in the late 1960s, reported: "The people in Fort Vermilion are very hard to describe, for they are interested for about one meeting and it is hard to get them to come back for another one. . . . Just when I think I have a good start the people seem to back out. When I talk to people they seem to be for it and when I approach somebody to call a small meeting then no one shows up."

In 1967 the Alberta Native Communications Society was formed to improve communication amongst themselves, a most critical element if they were to present a strong voice to government. Through these activities and organizations, it was hoped that "native groups [could] bring together the cultural base of the past and break into the dominant society for knowledge and means necessary for survival."

In Manitoba the Annual Conference of Indian and Metis sponsored by the Welfare Council of Winnipeg was the only voice to speak for social action for Native people in the province. In the past this meeting had concentrated on treaty rights and band councils, which had no relevance to the Metis. Although the Metis shared many of the same problems as the Indians, they felt they did not have the same advantages, so there was little communication between the two. In 1967 the Metis decided they needed a separate group and formally incorporated the Manitoba Metis Federation, with the Reverend Adam Cuthand as president. An attempt was made to bring all the Metis in the province together under one umbrella organization, with programs concentrating on economic and cultural problems. The priorities were to find employment and to improve housing conditions, as well as to reinforce and rebuild Metis identity and pride.

To ease the destitution of Metis who lived permanently in urban centres and to assist newcomers who were unfamiliar with city life, an Indian Metis Friendship Centre was opened in Winnipeg, with others following in Alberta and Saskatchewan in the early 1960s. In 1968 the Canadian Metis Society, which included Nonstatus Indians, was formed as an offshoot of the National Indian Brotherhood. Three years later the Native Council of Canada emerged with "the aim of achieving full Native (mixed and full-blood) participation of life in modern Canadian society."

As the Metis began to organize, the need to define who they were became ever more critical. Were they Indians who had been denied the rights of Indians? Were they white? Or were they somewhere in between? What were their greatest problems? By the end of the 1960s, a myriad of studies had been done on the Metis by various academics and government officials. They had been examined as individuals, including their personal characteristics, or as members of larger groups such as families, households, communities and organizations.

In spite of the quantity of information available, conditions had not improved.

Because of their entrepreneurial, independent and adaptive spirit, the Metis of the nineteenth century laid a solid groundwork for the Metis of the twentieth century. Some chose to leave their Indianness behind; others chose to reinforce it; still others chose to live in both worlds. The political organizations of the 1960s continued the battle to improve the economic situation of the Metis. But who the Metis were in a cultural sense could be understood only by looking at the individual lives of people in the general Metis population. Native heritage is only part of Metis identity. Legal status and social pressures, combined with independence and individuality, have defined the Metis as both Native and white. Historian Murray Dobbin recognized this when he said, "it was not so much blood that was mixed [in the Metis] . . . but two different worlds."

Chapter Five

Towards Recognition & Justice
1970 to 1985

When Prime Minister Pierre Trudeau announced a policy of multiculturalism in October 1971, he established that his government was willing to acknowledge the many ethnic identities in Canada. He stated that a sense of national identity could be engendered in people only when they had a strong sense of personal identity. Based on this policy and the funds provided to support it, the Metis were guaranteed survival as long as they took the responsibility of nurturing their identity in all aspects — economically, politically and culturally. But the Metis, who were still fighting the battles of unemployment, poverty, poor health and lack of education, had little time or energy to devote to culture or politics. At a conference on cultural education held some years later, the issue was stated succinctly: "culture is nice but right now my family needs food and my children need education."

But Metis culture is more than doing beadwork, playing the fiddle, dancing the Red River jig or having a particular set of spiritual beliefs. The desire to remain distinct from Indian and white worlds and to gain strength from both elements of their heritage has established a bond among some Metis, and

their large kinship network has strengthened their sense of identity. Through educational and cultural programs, political organizations of recent years have created an awareness of who the Metis were in history and who they are today. The essence and strength of their identity is that they have never been one unified body slotted into only one niche. Rather, through their diverse talents and strong individuality, they have filled many places in the Canadian mosaic. The realization of this will lead to the further development of Metis literature, visual art, music and drama.

The l'Assomption sash, the one item from their colourful history that was identified with them, has been adopted by some groups as a symbol of their identity, but the idea of defining themselves by the clothes they wear has become a source of humour. If a Metis encountered another dressed in a buckskin jacket and sash, he would say, "Oh, are you applying for a government grant?" At other times, the wearing of a suit and tie has drawn angry reactions, and one frustrated Metis responded: "What [do] . . . you expect me to wear? a a coon-skin cap?" There has never been one singularly defined Metis "costume," least of all one stereotyped by folklore

Pages 136/137: A Metis teadance in northern Alberta. Photograph by Doug Curran, Edmonton.

The entrance gates in the early years of an annual sports and cultural event held at Batoche. Now called Metis Heritage Days, it draws Metis people from all over the West. Courtesy Aboriginal Multi-Media Society of Alberta

Beadwork continues to be a popular creative expression for many Metis women, as well as providing a limited source of income for them. Courtesy New Breed, SNCC

and commercialism. Sometimes clothing and decorative items are borrowed from other groups and, when worn together by a Metis with imagination, reflect Jim Brady's proud description of his people: "We are born individualists."

The 1970s saw the maturation of many of the Metis organizations and the creation of new ones, with a great deal of time and energy spent documenting land claims and living conditions. They presented numerous briefs to the federal and provincial governments on the topics of education, health and employment, but throughout this work, problems of funding continued to plague the organizations. In earlier years, Norris and Brady had argued against the acceptance of government funds, as they thought it would compromise them. But the 1970s were a different era from the 1930s, when the Metis in Alberta and Saskatchewan had first organized. To make themselves heard, they had now to learn about communications and the media. Also, their briefs had to be thoroughly researched, prepared and presented in a professional manner. These things all cost money and if the Metis and other Native groups wanted to be effective in the 1970s, government funding was necessary.

In Alberta, the Federation of Metis Settlements, started in the 1970s, did manage to survive mainly on membership fees. With a goal to achieve "autonomy and self-determination" for the communities, the federation strengthened communication and began a major research program to clarify their status under the Metis Betterment Act. But the most critical action was the launching of a suit against the provincial government

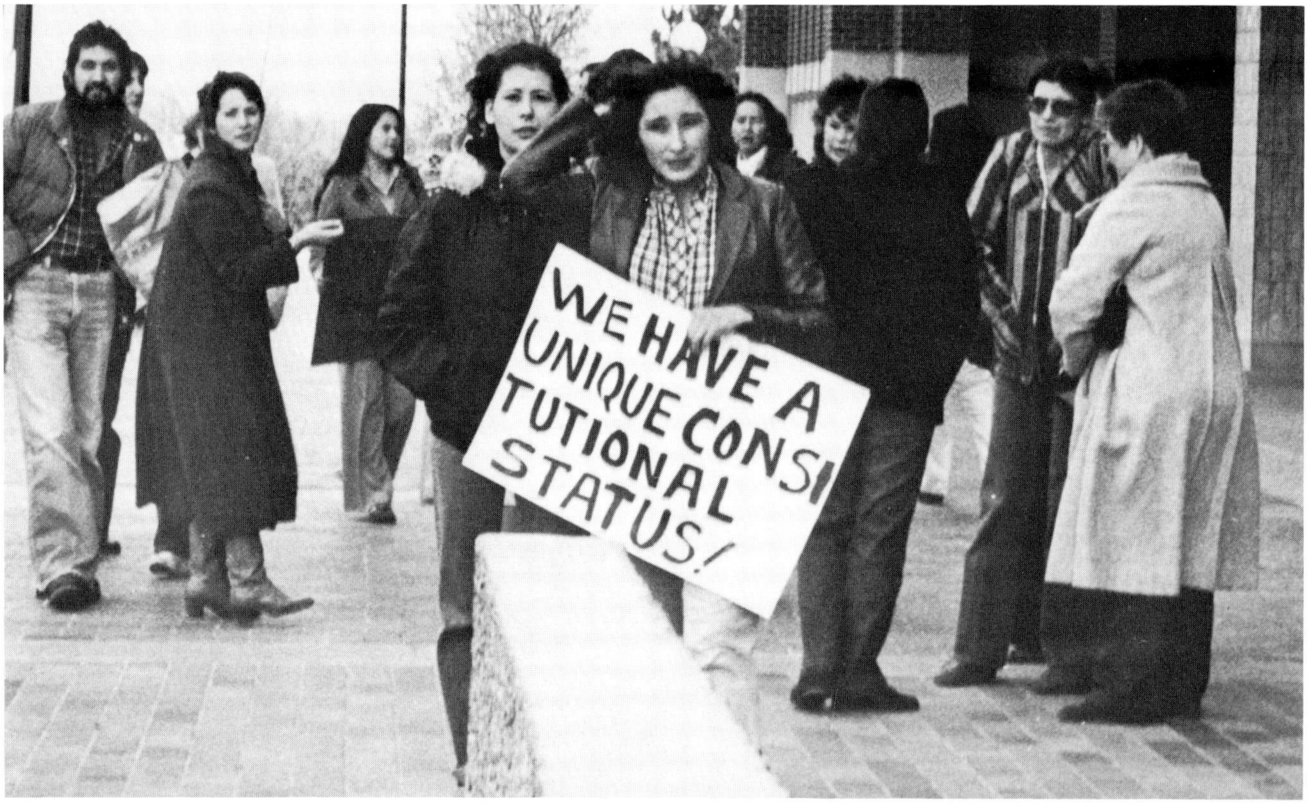
WE HAVE A
UNIQUE CONSI
TUTIONAL
STATUS!

WE ARE the
LANDlORDs
this Country!
TRUDEAU: your
RENT IS OVER

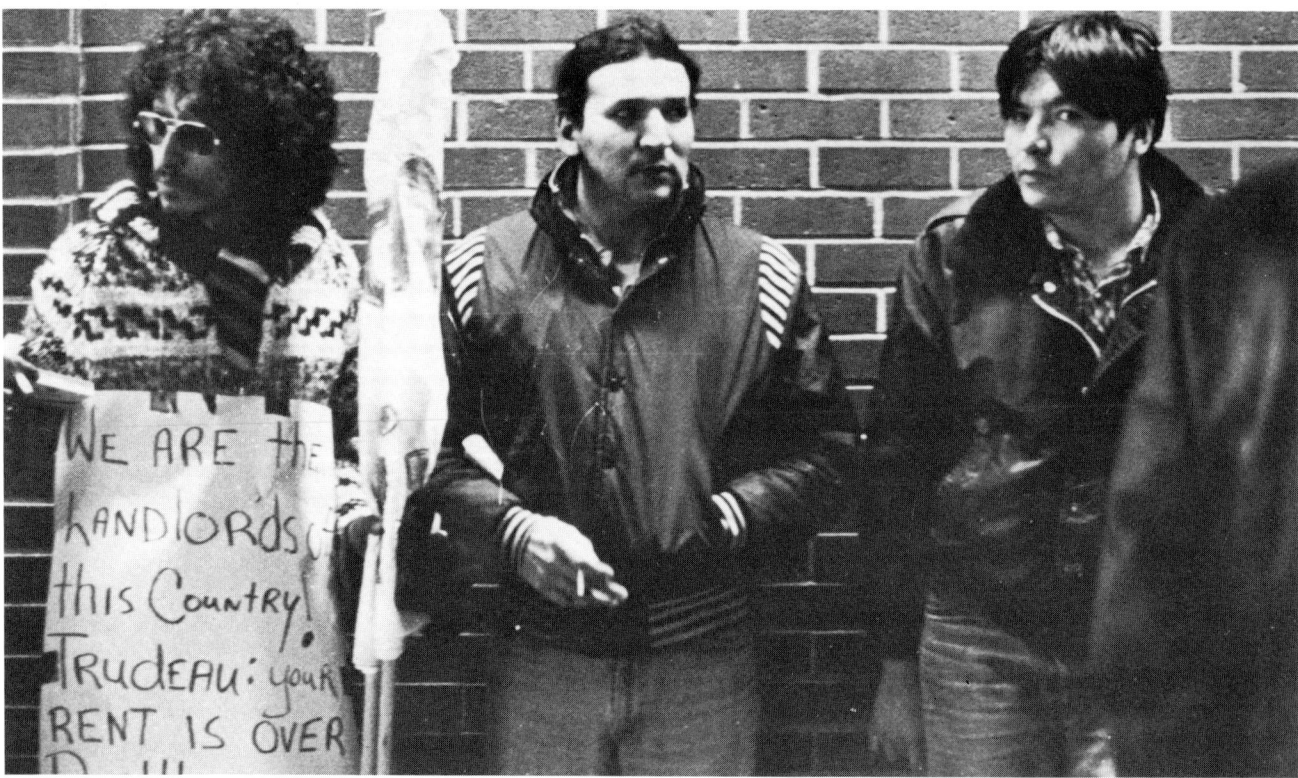

in 1974 to obtain the profits from natural resources, particularly oil and gas, on the settlements. The case is still in the courts and it will probably be several years before the issue is settled. In 1979 the files of some Metis settlements that were being reviewed by the counsel for the federation were confiscated by the Department of Social Services at the request of the counsel to the Crown in the court case for the purposes of auditing. The provincial ombudsman investigated the incident and concluded that an official apology should be made to the federation by the provincial government, but this was never done. He also suggested that the Metis Development Branch, which administered the Metis settlements, did not belong under the direction of the Department of Social Services, and in 1980 it was shifted to the Department of Municipal Affairs.

All the Metis associations fought during the 1970s to organize education programs designed to make what Metis children are taught in the schools more relevant to how they live. Many of these programs are now being implemented by government school boards.

The actions of Metis associations in Manitoba, Saskatchewan and Alberta have brought them closer to a sense of their own identity and unity. They have moved a long way from a statement made at the beginning of the decade: "There is a sector of society which is legally referred to as 'Indian' and which can prove its lineage by a demoralizing device known as a 'treaty number.'... We, their brothers and sisters, who through some accident of history do not possess an identifying number, are left unable to produce identity."

In 1980 the Canadian government concentrated its energies towards the patriation of the Constitution, and a parliamentary commission was formed to hear submissions from various groups who wished to present their views about this vital document. Jim Sinclair, spokesperson for the Native Council of Canada, representing Metis and Non-status Indians, appeared before the commission and expressed the implications for his people: "This consitutional process has considerable merit. Inherent in this process is the opportunity to provide the

foundation wherein our people can begin to settle the fundamental outstanding issues which have made the Metis and Nonstatus Indians the forgotten people of Canada." He continued with a warning that "we [the Metis] will never surrender our identity as a separate and distinct people within the Canadian mosaic.... We have a significant piece of unfinished business that strikes at the foundation of Canadian society."

A list of twenty Metis rights were drawn up and presented to the commission, under the categories of land and natural resources, culture and education, language and communication, eco-

Facing page, top: Metis demonstrators in Regina during the constitutional talks. Courtesy New Breed, *SNCC*

Facing page, bottom: A demonstration held by the Association of Metis and Non-Status Indians of Saskatchewan in Regina during a visit from Prime Minister Pierre Trudeau.

This page: Raising their voices in songs drawn from their Native roots, Metis demand recognition in the constitutional process. Courtesy New Breed, *SNCC*

nomics and social development, and special political status. These rights included: recognition of the special status of the Metis as Native people; recognition and protection of cultural differences; self-government and self-determination; a just settlement for land loss; education of their children in their own language, customs and traditions; representation in all legislative assemblies; adequate housing, and access to the rights and privileges enjoyed by all citizens.

After long and heated debates among representatives of the federal government, provincial governments and national Native organizations, the Canada Act was passed. In it the "existing aboriginal and treaty rights" of Native people were recognized, and significantly, the term "aboriginal people of Canada" was identified to include "Indian, Inuit and Métis." In earlier drafts of the Constitution, the various clauses dealing with aboriginal peoples had not identified who they were. Along with the other Native peoples of Canada, the Metis were concerned about what "aboriginal rights" as written in the Constitution really meant, and all agreed to hold a series of First Ministers' Conferences to define and identify them.

The Metis of Saskatchewan objected to the constitutional package accepted by the Native Council of Canada (NCC), claiming that because they had broken off from the NCC they were not represented at the constitutional talks. Later they joined with the Metis associations of British Columbia, Alberta and Manitoba to form the Metis National Council. It was clear to these groups that the concerns represented in the NCC, which

Facing page: A young Metis boy proudly wears his first-prize ribbon for winning a dogsled race in North Battleford, Saskatchewan. Courtesy New Breed, SNCC

Top: Many Metis remain devout Catholics, participating regularly in pilgrimages to sacred sites such as Lac Ste. Anne in western Alberta. Courtesy Aboriginal Multi-Media Society of Alberta

Bottom: Hauling wood on a Metis colony in northern Alberta. Photograph by Doug Curran, Edmonton

Metis firefighters in northern Alberta. These men often work for limited renumeration under dangerous conditions. Courtesy Doug Curran, Edmonton

included a recognition of pre-Confederation treaties (something the Metis had never signed), were quite different from those of the Metis.

In March 1983 the first of a series of Constitutional Conferences presented the Metis with an opportunity to outline their main objectives for a political settlement: to gain a land base and a right to self-government. They stressed they were looking for partnership in Canada rather than any form of sovereignty.

At the second conference held in April 1984, the main issue was a clarification of who the Metis were and are. The Metis National Council presented a definition that included three criteria: self-identification as a Metis, community acceptance of an individual as a Metis, and if necessary, historical or legal proof that such an individual has "held himself/herself out to be a Metis." The council insisted that Metis must be defined on the basis of biology, common history and culture and political consciousness, and also requested that an enumeration be done by the federal government under this definition. But the council's proposal was rejected, and it was agreed that identification of the Metis would be a main agenda item at the next meeting, scheduled for 1985.

Harvesting wild rice in northern Saskatchewan provides a limited income for many Metis. Courtesy New Breed, SNCC

So the discussion, as always, keeps coming full circle back to the old question of exactly who the Metis are. At least one aspect of their identity has been defined by the declaration in the Constitution that they have rights as aboriginal people within Canada. The Metis themselves know who they are; now they must convince the politicians.

Inherent in their inclusion in the definition of "aboriginal people," the Metis claim, is that they have aboriginal rights, "those rights which native people retain as a result of their original possession of the soil." They do not think that these rights were extinguished by the scrip that the government gave to the Metis, and contemporary Metis have bitterly criticized the entire scrip program, suggesting that it was designed to suit the needs of the government rather than to give a just settlement to the Metis. They believe that though the government implemented the scrip program to "extinguish" Metis rights, it did not do so because most Metis took money scrip. Further, they claim that the government did not act in good faith, as it allowed speculation to run rampant during the scrip program, and many Metis lost their land very quickly after receiving it.

However the Metis claim to aboriginal

147

rights is viewed, the cruel fact remains that a large number of them are still relegated to a life of poverty and despair. Their situation will someday improve, because the Metis have tenaciously held on to their identity as a new nation for more than two hundred years in Canada, and they refuse to disappear. Although a historian once said of Louis Riel and his people, "he died on the gallows and his nation died with him," an old Metis grandmother said to her grandchild, "Because they killed Riel, they think they have killed us too, but some day my girl, it will be different."

Based on their ability to organize and work together in times of necessity, a tradition that dates back to the days of the buffalo hunts, as well as the effectiveness of their arguments in discussion at First Ministers' Conferences, the question of Metis rights will eventually be settled. As astute politicians, they hope to gain what legal debates have failed to achieve and recent cultural activities have begun to nurture.

Although the Metis possess personal identities that nevertheless reflect common values and attitudes, their desire for freedom and individuality has remained their most distinctive characteristic. During times of trouble and threats to their way of life or to their survival, they have rallied to form a politically strong voice — however short-lived — to achieve a common goal. Their heritage, springing from the Native and European peoples of Canada, ensures them a unique place in the history of this land.

Facing page: A Metis fiddler. Photograph by Doug Curran, Edmonton

Notes

INTRODUCTION
THE METIS PEOPLE

10 When Louis Riel . . . : Association of Metis and Non-Status Indians of Saskatchewan, *Louis Riel*, viii.

10 Either the Metis . . . : Flanagan, *Louis 'David' Riel*, 173.

10 Some historians claim . . . : Sealey and Lussier, *The Metis*, 1.

11 Initially, the mixed-blood . . . : Foster, "The Metis," 86.

11 Another term . . . : Sealey and Lussier, *The Metis*, 14.

12 "we're not helf [sic] men . . . ": Hatt, Hobart and Hatt, "Ninety-Nine Years," 5.

12 "a merry, light-hearted . . . ": Milton and Cheadle, *The North-West Passage*, 41–42.

12 "pursuit of husbandry . . . ": Wallace, ed., *John McLean's Notes*, 378.

12 *o-tee-paym-soo-wuk*: Alberta Federation of Metis Settlement Associations, Anderson and Anderson, *The Metis People*, 2.

12 "Unlike many other . . . ": Sealey and Lussier, *The Metis*, 169.

12 "polyglot jabber": Gilman, Gilman and Stultz, *The Red River Trails*, 14.

12 *tout mêlé*: Douaud, "Canadian Metis Identity," 83.

12 "a fine broad Scotch . . . ": Gilman, Gilman and Stultz, *The Red River Trails,*, 14.

12 *michif*: Crawford, "What Sort of Thing Is Michif?" (Work paper, conference, Newberry Library, 1981), 1.

12 By the nineteenth century . . . : Sealey and Lussier, *The Metis*, 14.

14 "easier to define . . . ": Sawchuk, *The Metis of Manitoba*, 39.

14 "Canada's galleries . . . ": Alberta Federation of Metis Settlement Associations, *Metisism*, 45.

14 Thus, much of what . . . : Brasser, "In Search of Metis Art," 1.

14 "There never was . . . ": Campbell, *Halfbreed*, 26.

15 (Current figures . . .): *Aboriginal Multi-Media Society of Alberta*, 15 April 1983, 7.

15 "caught in the vacuum . . . ": McKay, "The Non-People," 18.

15 "they are Metis . . . ": Sawchuk, *The Metis of Manitoba*, 10.

15 "the true spirit . . . ": Daniels, "A Declaration," as quoted in Driben, "The Nature of Metis Claims," 85.

CHAPTER ONE
A FREE AND INDEPENDENT PEOPLE: TO 1885

19 A blue capote . . . : Nute, *The Voyageur*, 13.

19 These men readily . . . : Sealey and Lussier, *The Metis*, 25–26.

19 These York boats . . . : *New Breed*, July 1982, 10.

20 "Captain General . . . ": Stanley, *The Birth of Western Canada*, 11.

20 "assert their claim . . . ": ibid.

20 That same year . . . : Sealey and Lussier, *The Metis*, 41–42.

20 "raise the moral . . . ": ibid., 55.

21 The first Roman Catholic . . . : MacGregor, *Father Lacombe*, 27.

21 The Reverend J. West . . . : Boon, *The Anglican Church*, 1–21.

21 Several years later . . . : Morton, *Manitoba*, 71 and MacGregor, *Father Lacombe*, 35.

21 In 1851 the first . . . : Van Kirk, "What If Mama Is an Indian?" in *The Developing West*, ed. Foster, 127.

21 The great buffalo hunts . . . : based largely on Ross, *The Red River Settlement*, 241–74.

22 "half-wagon, half-man": Sealey and Lussier, *The Metis*, 21.

22 The cart came . . . : Morton, *Manitoba*, 57.

22 The carts were . . . : see Gilman, Gilman and Stultz, *The Red River Trails*, 14–16, for a thorough discussion of the carts.

22 "inelegent [sic] box": Maclean, "A Tribute to the Red River Cart," 34.

22 "lashed to the cart . . . ": Gilman, Gilman and Stultz, *The Red River Trails*, 15.

22 "Each cart . . . ": Maclean, "A Tribute to the Red River Cart," 35.

22 "hellish"; "your blood run cold"; "the scraping . . . ": as quoted in Gilman, Gilman and Stultz, *The Red River Trails*, 16.

22 "its own . . . "; "drawn through bogs": ibid.

22 "strong on . . . ": ibid., 15.

22 In winter . . . : Southesk, *Saskatchewan*, 293.

22 A cart could . . . : Gilman, Gilman and Stultz, *The Red River Trails*, 15.

22 "The carts . . . ": ibid.

23 "1. No buffalo . . . ": Ross, *The Red River Settlement*, 249–500.

24 "tended with all . . . ": Wallace, ed., *John McLean's Notes*, 375.

26 "polkas, galops . . . ": Healy, *Women of the Red River*, 217.

27 "a brilliant accompaniment . . . ": Nute, *The*

150

27 *Voyageur*, 84.
27 "cry of the loon . . . " : Sealey and Lussier, *The Metis*, 18–19.
27 "all the appearance . . . " : Ross, *The Red River Settlement*, 196.
27 "passionately fond of . . . " ; "great tobacco-smokers" ; "great tea drinkers" : ibid., 193.
27 "The cariole . . . " : Kane, *Wanderings of an Artist*, 271.
27 "gay painted cariole[s]" : Ross, *The Red River Settlement*, 196.
27 "Russian bells . . . " : Ralph, *On Canada's Frontier*, 229.
27 "gaudily decorated . . . " : Kane, *Wanderings of an Artist*, 270.
27 On their horses . . . : Southesk, *Saskatchewan*, 45.
27 "Beribboned and prancing . . . " : Sealey and Lussier, *The Metis*, 19.
27 Trotting matches . . . : Ross, *The Red River Settlement*, 196.
27 "besetting sins . . . " : Milton and Cheadle, *The North-West Passage*, 42.
28 "but they are . . . " : Ross, *The Red River Settlement*, 195.
28 "a fellow with . . . " ; "glib ice . . . " ; "Who is . . . " ; "this glittering . . . " : ibid., 196–97.
29 "notable mainly for . . . " : Gilman, Gilman and Stultz, *The Red River Trails*, 14.
29 "restrained by no . . . " : Tytler, *The Northern Coasts*, 314.
29 l'Assomption sash: see Barbeau, "Assomption Sash."
29 "not remarkable . . . " : Southesk, *Saskatchewan*, 348.
30 "chiefly of the . . . " : Ross, *The Red River Settlement*, 191.
30 Young women . . . : Dusenberry, "The Metis of Montana," 90.
30 "bright-coloured skirts . . . " : Milton and Cheadle, *The North-West Passage*, 69.
30 They had more . . . : Duncan, "The Metis and Production of Embroidery," 6.
30 "Over each column . . . " : as quoted in Morier, "Metis Decorative Art," 31.
31 "gossiping parties" : Ross, *The Red River Settlement*, 193.
31 Never afraid to . . . : see Thayer, "Some Examples of 'Red River Half-Breed' Art."
31 "the gay fashion" ; "where taste . . . " : Southesk, *Saskatchewan*, 171.
31 "helped to introduce . . . " : Ewers, *Indian Life,*, 66.
31 *hiverants*: see Baldwin, "Wintering Villages," Land Claims Research Project, 1979–80, Metis Association of Alberta, M5713, Glenbow Archives.
31 "forty to fifty . . . " ; "The doors are . . . " : Blaireau to the Editor, *The Manitoban*, 5 January 1872, M477f3, Glenbow Archives.

32 "an armoury of . . . " : as quoted in Baldwin, "Wintering Villages," Land Claims Research Project, 1979–80, Metis Association of Alberta, M5713, Glenbow Archives.
32 "Le commerce est . . . " : Ross, *The Red River Settlement*, 376.
35 "[a] line extending far . . . " : Gilman, Gilman and Stultz, *The Red River Trails*, 14.
35 "skin garments . . . " : ibid.
36 At about that time . . . : Metis Association of Alberta et al., *Metis Land Rights in Alberta*, 12.
36 In the tradition . . . : Stanley, *The Birth of Western Canada*, 69. Much of this discussion of the first rebellion is based on 67–143.
36 Comité National des Métis: Sealey and Lussier, *The Metis*, 78.
36 "force the Canadian . . . " : Stanley, *The Birth of Western Canada*, 71.
36 The provisional government . . . : Sealey and Lussier, *The Metis*, 83.
39 The Alexander Ross family . . . : see Van Kirk, "What If Mama Is an Indian?"
39 "an annoyed member . . . " ; "Metis people do not . . . " : MacEwan, *Metis Makers of History*, 95.
40 Distribution of the land . . . : this discussion is based largely on Sealey and Lussier, *The Metis*, 96–98.
43 Gabriel Dumont . . . : see Woodcock, *Gabriel Dumont*, 90.
43 Without question . . . : Flanagan, *Riel and the Rebellion*, 4.
44 A delegation consisting of . . . : much of this discussion is based on Stanley, *The Birth of Western Canada*, 243–68.
45 " 'folies de grandeurs' . . . " : Flanagan, *Louis 'David' Riel*, 57.
47 It was in keeping . . . : see Dobbin, *The One-and-a-half-Men*, 25.

CHAPTER TWO
CHANGE AND THE STRUGGLE TO SURVIVE: 1885 TO 1920

56 "Already undermined . . . " : Dobbin, *The One-and-a-half-Men*, 25.
57 "the company . . . " : as quoted in Lalonde, "The North-West Rebellion," 101.
57 "idle, dissipated . . . " : Butler, *The Great Lone Land*, 362.
57 "while he was . . . " ; "there is no one . . . " : Ralph, *On Canada's Frontier*, 219.
59 "I have often been struck . . . " : Blaireau to the Editor, *The Manitoban*, 5 January 1872, M477f3, Glenbow Archives.
61 "opposed to Indians . . . " : ibid.
61 "must feel rather ashamed . . . " : Van Kirk, "What If Mama Is an Indian?" 129.
64 Generally, however, the size . . . : Payment,

"History of Batoche Village," 10.
64 Many Metis women . . . : Calihoo, "Early Life in Lac St. Anne," 10.
64 Diversity became . . . : see Sawchuk, *The Metis of Manitoba*.
65 "I left my old home . . . " : Calihoo to Cochrane, 25 February 1939, M. Loggie Papers, D971.23.L832, Glenbow Archives.
66 "While the meat . . . " : as quoted in Anick, "The Metis of the South Saskatchewan," vol. 1, Report no. 364, 1976, Parks Canada.
67 "short northwestern gun" : Ewers, "The North West Trade Gun," 7.
67 "an old flint rifle . . . " : Southesk, *Saskatchewan*, 199.
67 "prevent [them] . . . " : Russell, *Explorations*, 180.
67 "tuppies" : Osgood, "Great Bear Lake Indians," 65.
67 "the finest . . . " ; "she turned . . . " ; "the men tell me . . . " : Seton, *The Arctic Prairies*, 281–82.
68 Numbers of Metis . . . : all quotations in this paragraph, ibid., 92–93.
70 "cast off garments . . . " ; "However sordid . . . " : ibid., 41.
70 "in practically every line . . . " : Mason, "Indians of the Great Slave Lake," 21 and quoted in Thompson, "Metis Decorative Art," 41.
70 Perhaps some . . . : see Duncan, "Production of Embroidery."
72 "for there are but a few . . . " : Rutten to Morris. Files, Royal Ontario Museum.
72 To encourage the Metis . . . : see Giraud, "The Western Metis."
72 "were strict Sabbatarians . . . " : Seton, *The Arctic Prairies*, 19.
72 Other special days . . . : see Payment, "History of Batoche Village," 83.
73 "half-breeds . . . " ; "as if they . . . " : as quoted in Sealey and Lussier, "Ethnicity," 15.
73 The word "scrip" . . . : much of this discussion is taken from Metis Association of Alberta, Research Report on Land Claims, 1978, M5848, Glenbow Archives; Metis Association of Alberta et al., *Metis Land Rights in Alberta*; and Taylor, "Metis Claims."
73 Most Metis took . . . : Metis Association of Alberta et al., *Metis Land Rights in Alberta*, 104.
74 "in the North West . . . " : ibid., 119.
74 "the biggest social event . . . " : Sharpe, "Half-Breed Scrip," Land Claims Research Final Report, 18 April 1978, 72, M5848, Glenbow Archives.
75 "The town had . . . " : *Edmonton Bulletin*, 4 July 1885.
75 "A dozen beer saloons . . . " : Sanders, Anglican Church Records, 137,70.387, Provincial Archives of Alberta.
78 "a land reserve . . . " : Metis Association of Alberta et al., *Metis Land Rights in Alberta*, 164; see ibid., 159–85, for much of the discussion about St. Paul des Métis.
82 "Private Patrick Riel . . . " : *Metis News*, 27 November 1972, 4.
82 More information is . . . : see Dempsey, "The Indians and World War One," for a discussion about Indians in the First World War.

CHAPTER THREE
POVERTY AND A PASSION FOR POLITICS: 1920 TO 1949

92 "we used to paddle . . . " : *New Breed*, December 1983, 12.
93 Hundreds of thousands . . . : Groenland, "Scrip Scandal," Research Report on Land Claims, 1978, Metis Association of Alberta, M5848, Glenbow Archives.
94 During this period . . . : Hatt, "The Canadian Metis," 4–5.
94 "an elderly gentleman . . . " : Dion, *My Tribe the Crees*, 145–46.
96 Her father, Pierre Poitras . . . : Bellegarde, interview with author, June 1983.
96 Many Metis women . . . : ibid.
96 "He was in jail . . . " : Campbell, *Halfbreed*, 55.
96 "One thing about our people . . " : ibid., 51.
96 "on sticks . . . " ; "really delicious . . . " : ibid., 76.
97 Although most Metis . . . : ibid., 17.
97 Brady's library . . . : Dobbin, *The One-and-a-half Men*, 15, 196.
97 Pete Tomkins probably . . . : Hatt, "The Ewing Commission," 5.
97 "the half-breed is . . . " : Report of the Royal Commission on the Condition of the Halfbreed Population of the Province of Alberta, 9.
97 "But in 1931 . . . " : Dobbin, *The One-and-a-half Men*, 59.
97 Recognizing that . . . : ibid.
97 One of these . . . : ibid., 77.
97 "radicals": ibid., 76.
97 The first annual convention . . . : much of the discussion about the organization of the Metis Association of Alberta in the 1930s is based on Metis Association of Alberta et al., *Metis Land Rights in Alberta*, and Hatt, "The Ewing Commission."
97 Further recognition . . . : much of the discussion about the Ewing Commission is based on the Report of the Royal Commission on the Condition of the Halfbreed Population of the Province of Alberta, 9.
97 "to inquire into . . . " : Hatt, "The Ewing Commission," 1.
99 "if he has . . . " ; "the life of . . . " : Report of the Royal Commission on the Condition of the Halfbreed Population of the Province of Alberta, 14.

101 "for the purpose . . ." : Metis Association of Alberta et al., *Metis Land Rights in Alberta*, 193.
101 "elementary"; "while the girls . . ." : Report of the Royal Commission on the Condition of the Halfbreed Population of the Province of Alberta, 7.
101 "remain a good . . ." : as quoted in Sharpe, "Half-Breed Scrip," Land Claims Research Final Report, 18 April 1978, 303, M5848, Glenbow Archives.
104 "revealing their . . ." : Dobbin, *The One-and-a-half Men*, 123.
105 "the lack of . . ." : Dion to Brady, Dion Papers, M331, box 2, Glenbow Archives.
105 "the association was created . . ." : as quoted in Dobbin, *The One-and-a-half Men*, 135.
105 In the mid-1930s . . . : this discussion is drawn largely from a series of articles published in *New Breed*, August to December 1978.
105 "true halfbreeds . . ." : *New Breed*, October 1978.
107 "peacemakers, negotiators . . ." : Noonan and Hodges, "The Saskatchewan Metis," 34.
107 "train and fit . . ." : *New Breed*, October 1978, 14.
107 Governments in both . . . : Sealey and Lussier, *The Metis*, 153.
107 In 1945 . . . : see Valentine, Confidential Report, The Metis, Department of Natural Resources, for a discussion of the Fur Marketing Board and block conservation system.
110 "content to grow . . ."; "very proud . . ." : ibid., 94.
110 Another program . . . : see Symington, "Metis Rehabilitation," for a discussion of Green Lake.
110 Henry Pelletier . . . : all quotations in paragraph from Dobbin, interview with Pelletier, 17 March 1978, A1324, Saskatchewan Archives Board.
110 "unutterable filth . . ."; "after a while . . ." : Symington, "Metis Rehabilitation," 134, 137.
111 "After supper . . ." : Campbell, *Halfbreed*, 51–52.
111 Mrs. Lena Bellegarde . . . : Bellegarde, interview with author, June 1983.
111 Pierre Falcon . . . : see MacLeod, *Songs of Old Manitoba*, 1–4.
111 "black, ankle-length . . ." : Campbell, *Halfbreed*, 15.
111 "the living-room . . ." : ibid., 20.
112 "there was . . ." : ibid.
112 "On a cold winter night . . ." : ibid.
113 Sister Leduc . . . : Sister Leduc, interview with author, August 1983.
115 According to some sources . . . : Redbird, *We Are Metis*, 28.
115 Metis leaders . . . : Dobbin, *The One-and-a-half Men*, 138, 145.
117 "our true destiny . . ." : as quoted in ibid., 136.
117 Spurred by the . . . : see Dempsey, "The Indians and World War One."
117 "Canada's leading producer . . ." : Buckley, "Trapping and Fishing," 58.
117 "in a pleasant . . ."; "their intellectual attitudes . . ." : as quoted in Dobbin, *The One-and-a-half Men*, 140.
119 Their common experience . . . : Valentine, Confidential Report, The Metis, Department of Natural Resources, 21.
119 The war involvement . . . : see Dobbin, *The One-and-a-half Men*, 177.

CHAPTER FOUR
REKINDLING THE FIRES: 1950 TO 1969

122 During the war . . . : Poitras, interview with author, June 1983.
122 The first major study . . . : see Lagasse, "Population of Indian Ancestry," for a detailed discussion of the report and its findings.
122 "living conditions . . ."; "a considerable degree . . ." : ibid., I:1.
123 "regret, perhaps guilt . . ." : ibid.
123 "recapture the spirit . . ." : ibid.
123 When the study . . . : ibid., I:2.
123 "he is a half-breed . . ." : ibid., I:56.
123 "a municipal official . . ." : ibid., I:153.
123 At the 1958 meeting . . . : ibid., I:77.
123 "language, physical appearance . . ." : ibid., I:4.
124 Across the prairies . . . : ibid., I:68.
124 "mid way between . . ." : ibid., I:68.
124 "rough log cabins . . ." : Valentine, Confidential Report, The Metis, Department of Natural Resources, 12–13.
127 "The walls are . . ." : ibid.
127 "untidiness is . . ." : ibid., 14.
127 Although Lagasse . . . : Lagasse, "Population of Indian Ancestry" I:26–31.
127 For example . . . : Author's notes, July 1982.
127 "gorgeous sky blue . . ." : Seton, *The Arctic Prairies*, 91.
129 In card games . . : Valentine, Confidential Report, The Metis, Department of Natural Resources, 24–25.
129 At Green lake . . . : see Symington, "Metis Rehabilitation."
129 At one dance . . . : Johnston, interview with author, April 1984.
130 "kissing in the . . ."; "My father continued . . ." : as quoted in Sealey and Lussier, *The Metis*, 57.
130 On New Year's Day . . . : Various people, interviews with author, November 1982.
130 "that might find . . ." : Card, Hirabayashi and French, *The Metis in Alberta Society*, 13.
130 "I know what . . ." : ibid., 289.
131 The problems of poor housing . . . : ibid., 313.
132 "discuss the issues . . ." : Dobbin, *The One-and-a-half Men*, 201.

132 In September 1964 . . . : see ibid., 201–23.
133 "need for unity . . . " : ibid., 222.
133 Their diet was lacking . . . : Hatt, Hobart and Hatt, "Ninety-Nine Years," 313.
133 "It is the white people's . . . " : ibid., 332–34.
133 "frustrated and disgusted" : ibid., 325.
134 From 1967 to 1972 . . . : Metis Association of Alberta et al., *Metis Land Rights in Alberta*, 5.
134 "The people . . . " : Desjarlais, Field Report, 12 October 1969, Metis Association of Alberta Files, Glenbow Archives.
134 "native groups . . . " : Metis Association of Alberta, "A Proposal for Progress," 4.
134 In Manitoba . . . : Sawchuk, *The Metis of Manitoba*, 45–67.
134 "the aim of achieving . . . " : Douaud, "Canadian Metis Identity," 77.
135 "it was not so much . . . " : Dobbin, *The One-and-a-half Men*, 18.

CHAPTER FIVE
TOWARDS RECOGNITION AND JUSTICE: 1970 TO 1985

138 "culture is nice . . . " : Various people, interviews with author, November 1982.
139 "Oh, are you . . . " : as quoted in Redbird, *We Are Metis*, 33.
139 "What [do] . . . " : as quoted in Sawchuck, *The Metis of Manitoba*, 40.
141 "We are born individualists" : as quoted in Dobbin, *The One-and-a-half Men*, 133.
141 "autonomy and self-determination" : Metis Association of Alberta et al., *Metis Land Rights in Alberta*, 207. Much of this discussion is based on 206–10.
143 "There is a sector . . . " : as quoted in Sawchuck, *The Metis of Manitoba*, 33.
143 "This constitutional . . . " : *New Breed*, December 1980, 4.
143 "we [the Metis] . . . " : ibid., 6.
143 A list of twenty . . . : *Forgotten People*, March 1981, 6; *New Breed*, December 1980, 4–6.
144 "existing aboriginal and treaty rights" ; "aboriginal people of Canada" ; "Indian, Inuit and Métis" : Flanagan, "The Case Against," 315.
146 In March 1983 . . . : see *New Breed*, February to April 1983.
146 The Metis National Council . . . ; "held himself/herself . . . " : ibid., March 1984.
147 "those rights which . . . " : Driben, "The Nature of Metis Claims," 188.
149 "he died . . . " : as quoted in Association of Metis and Non-Status Indians of Saskatchewan, *Louis Riel*, viii.
149 "Because they killed . . . " : Campbell, *Halfbreed*, 15.

Bibliography

PUBLISHED SOURCES

Alberta Federation of Metis Settlement Associations. *Metisism: A Canadian Identity*. Edmonton: Alberta Federation of Metis Settlement Associations, 1982.

Alberta Federation of Metis Settlement Associations, Daniel R. Anderson and Alda M. Anderson. *The Metis People of Canada: A History*. Edmonton: Alberta Federation of Metis Settlement Associations, 1978.

Association of Metis and Non-Status Indians of Saskatchewan. *Louis Riel: Justice Must Be Done*. Winnipeg: Manitoba Metis Federation Press, 1979.

Barbeau, Marius. "Assomption Sash." *National Museum of Canada Bulletin*, no. 93. N.p., Department of Mines and Resources, n.d.

Boon, T. C. B. *The Anglican Church from the Bay to the Rockies*. Toronto: Ryerson Press, 1962.

Brasser, T. J. "Metis Artisans; Their Teachers and Their Pupils." *The Beaver* (Autumn 1975).

Brown, Jennifer S. H. *Strangers in Blood: Fur Trade Company Families in Indian Country*. Vancouver: University of British Columbia Press, 1980.

Buckley, Helen. "Trapping and Fishing in the Economy of Northern Saskatchewan." Report no. 3. Saskatoon: University of Saskatchewan, Research Division, Center for Community Studies, 1962.

Butler, William Francis. *The Great Lone Land*. Toronto: Musson Book Co., 1924.

Calihoo, Victoria. "Early Life in Lac St. Anne and St. Albert in the 1870s." *The Pioneer West* 2 (1970): 7–10.

Campbell, Maria. *Halfbreed*. Toronto: McClelland and Stewart, 1973.

Card, B. Y., G. K. Hirabayashi and C. L. French. *The Metis in Alberta Society*. Report on Project A. Edmonton: University of Alberta, 1963.

Cowie, Isaac. *The Company of Adventurers*. Toronto: William Briggs, 1913.

Dempsey, James. "The Indians and World War One." *Alberta History* 31 (1983): 1–8.

Dion, Joseph F. *My Tribe the Crees*. Calgary: Glenbow-Alberta Institute, 1979.

Dobbin, Murray. *The One-and-a-half Men: The Story of Jim Brady and Malcolm Norris, Metis Patriots of the 20th Century*. Vancouver: New Star Books, 1981.

Douaud, Patrick C. "Canadian Metis Identity: A Pattern of Evolution." *Anthropos* 78 (1983): 71–88.

Driben, Paul. "The Nature of Metis Claims." *The Canadian Journal of Native Studies* 3, no. 1 (1983): 183–96.

Duncan, Kate Corbin. "The Metis and Production of Embroidery in the Subarctic." *The Museum of the Fur Trade* 17, no. 3 (1981): 1–7.

Dusenberry, V. "The Metis of Montana." In *The Red Man's West*, edited by Michael Kennedy. New York: Hastings House Publishers, 1965.

Ewers, John C. *Indian Life on the Upper Missouri*. Norman: University of Oklahoma Press, 1968.

———. "The North West Trade Gun." *Alberta Historical Review* 4, no. 2 (1956): 3–9.

Flanagan, Thomas. "The Case Against Metis Aboriginal Rights." *Canadian Public Policy* 9, no. 3 (1983): 314–25.

———. *Louis 'David' Riel: 'Prophet of the New World.'* Toronto: University of Toronto Press, 1979.

———. *Riel and the Rebellion: 1885 Reconsidered*. Saskatoon: Western Producer Prairie Books, 1983.

Foster, J. E. "The Metis: The People and the Term." *Prairie Forum* 3, no. 1 (1978): 79–90.

Gilman, Rhoda R., Carolyn Gilman and Deborah M. Stultz. *The Red River Trails*. St. Paul: Minnesota Historical Society, 1979.

Giraud, Marcel. "The Western Metis After the Insurrection." *Saskatchewan History* 9, no. 1 (1956): 1–15.

Glover, R. "York Boats." *The Beaver* (March 1949): 19–23.

Gunn, J. J. *Echoes of the Red*. Toronto: Macmillan Company of Canada, 1930.

Hatt, F. K. "The Canadian Metis: Recent Interpretations." *Canadian Ethnic Studies* 3, no. 1 (1971): 1–16.

———. "The Ewing Commission of Alberta: An Interpretive Study of the Public Aspects of Policy Making." Edmonton: University of Alberta, 1972.

Hatt, Fred K., C. Hobart and J. Hatt. "Ninety-Nine Years from Tomorrow." A report on research and reaction. Edmonton: University of Alberta, 1971.

Healy, W. J. *Women of the Red River*. Winnipeg: Russell, Lang & Co., 1923.

Heilbron, B. L. "Mayer and the Treaty of 1851." *Minnesota History* 22, no. 2 (June 1941): 133–56.

Jamieson, Frederick C. "The Edmonton Hunt." *The Pioneer West* no. 1 (1969).

Kane, Paul. *Wanderings of an Artist*. 1859. Reprint. Edmonton: Hurtig Publishers, Canadian Reprint Series, 1968.

Lalonde, André N. "The North-West Rebellion and Its Effects on Settlers and Settlement in the Canadian West." *Saskatchewan History* 27, no. 3 (1974): 95–102.

MacBeth, John. "The Social Customs and Amusements in the Early Days in the Red River Settlement and Rupert's Land." In *The Historical* and Scientific Society of Manitoba. Transaction no. 44. Winnipeg: Manitoba Free Press Print, 24 January 1893.

MacEwan, Grant. *Metis Makers of History*. Saskatoon: Western Producer Prairie Books, 1981.

MacGregor, James G. *Father Lacombe*. Edmonton: Hurtig Publishers, 1975.

Maclean, John. "A Tribute to the Red River Cart." *Alberta History* 31, no. 1 (1983): 33–37.

MacLeod, Margaret Arnett. *Songs of Old Manitoba*. Toronto: Ryerson Press, 1960.

Mason, John A. *Notes on the Indians of the Great Slave Lake Area*. Yale University Publications in Anthropology, vol. 34. New Haven, Conn., 1946.

Metis Association of Alberta, Joe Sawchuk, Patricia Sawchuk and Theresa Ferguson. *Metis Land Rights in Alberta: A Political History*. Edmonton: Metis Association of Alberta, 1981.

Milton, Viscount, and W. B. Cheadle. *The North-West Passage By Land*. London: Cassell and Company, 1901.

Morier, Jan. "Metis Decorative Art and Its Inspiration." *Dawson and Hind* 8, no. 1 (n.d.): 28–32.

Morton, W. L. *Manitoba: A History*. Toronto: University of Toronto Press, 1957.

Nute, G. L. *The Voyageur*. 1931. Reprint. St. Paul: Minnesota Historical Society, 1955.

Osgood, Cornelius. "The Ethnography of the Great Bear Lake Indians." *National Museum of Canada Bulletin*, no. 70 (1932): 31–92.

Payment, Diane. "Structural and Settlement History of Batoche Village." *Canadian Historic Sites/Lieux historiques canadiens*. Manuscript Report no. 248. Ottawa: Parks Canada, Dept. of Indian and Northern Affairs, 1977.

Phillips, R. "Dreams and Designs: Iconographic Problems in Great Lakes Twined Bags." *Bulletin of the Detroit Institute of Arts* 62, no. 1 (1984). (In press).

Ralph, Julian. *On Canada's Frontier*. New York: Harper and Brothers, 1892.

Redbird, Duke. *We Are Metis*. Willowdale, Ontario: Ontario Metis and Non-Status Indian Association, 1980.

Ross, Alexander. *The Red River Settlement: Its Rise, Progress, and Present State*. Edmonton: Hurtig Publishers, 1972.

Russell, Frank. *Explorations in the Far North*. State University of Iowa, 1898.

Sawchuck, Joe. *The Metis of Manitoba: Reformulation of an Ethnic Identity*. Toronto: Peter Martin Associates, 1978.

Sealey, D. Bruce, and Antoine S. Lussier. *The Metis: Canada's Forgotten People*. Winnipeg: Manitoba Metis Federation Press, 1975.

Sealey, D. Bruce, and A. S. Lussier, eds. "Ethnicity and the Concept of Metisness." Papers presented at Pelletier-Lathlin Memorial Lecture Series. Brandon, Manitoba: Brandon University, 1979–80.

Seton, Ernest Thompson. *The Arctic Prairies*. Toronto: William Briggs, 1911.

Slobodin, Richard. *The Metis of the Mackenzie District*. Ottawa: Canadian Research Centre for Anthropology, St. Paul University, 1966.

Southesk, The Earl of. *Saskatchewan and the Rocky Mountains*. Edinburgh: Edmonston and Douglas, 1875.

Spaulding, Philip. "The Social Integration of a Northern Community: White Mythology and Metis Reality." In *A Northern Dilemma: Reference Papers*, edited by Arthur K. Davis. Bellingham: Western Washington State College, 1967.

Sprenger, Herman G. "The Metis Nation: Buffalo Hunting Vs. Agriculture in the Red River Settlement (Circa 1810–1870)." *Western Canadian Journal of Anthropology* 3, no. 1 (1972).

Stanley, George F. G. *The Birth of Western Canada: A History of the Riel Rebellions*. 2nd ed. Toronto: University of Toronto Press, 1960.

Symington, D. F. "Metis Rehabilitation." *Canadian Geographical Journal* 48, no. 4 (1953).

Taylor, John Leonard. "An Historical Introduction to Metis Claims in Canada." *The Canadian Journal of Native Studies* 3, no. 1 (1983).

Thayer, B. W. "Some Examples of 'Red River Half-Breed' Art." *Minnesota Archaeologist* 8 (April 1942).

Thomas, Lewis G., ed. *The Prairie West to 1905: A Canadian Sourcebook*. Toronto: Oxford University Press, 1975.

Thompson, Judy. "Turn-of-the-Century Metis Decorative Art from the Frederick Bell Collection." *American Indian Art* 8, no. 4 (1983).

Tytler, P. F. *The Northern Coasts of America and The Hudson's Bay Territories*. Edinburgh: T. Nelson & Sons, 1853.

Van Kirk, Sylvia M. "What If Mama Is an Indian? The Cultural Ambivalence of the Alexander Ross Family." In *The Developing West: Essays on Canadian History in Honour of Lewis H. Thomas*, edited by John E. Foster. Edmonton: University of Alberta Press, 1983.

Wallace, W. S., ed. *John McLean's Notes of a Twenty-Five Year's Service In The Hudson's Bay Territory*. Toronto: Champlain Society, 1932.

Woodcock, George. *Gabriel Dumont: The Metis Chief and His Lost World*. Edmonton: Hurtig Publishers, 1975.

UNPUBLISHED SOURCES

Alberta. Report of the Royal Commission on the Condition of the Halfbreed Population of the Province of Alberta, 1936.

Anick, N. "The Metis of the South Saskatchewan." Vol. 1, Report no. 364, Parks Canada, 1976.

Baldwin, Stuart J. "Wintering Villages of the Metis Hivernants: Documentary and Archaeological

Evidences." Land Claims Research Project, 1979–80, Metis Association of Alberta, M5713, Glenbow Archives.

Bellegarde, Lena. Interview with author. Fort Qu'Appelle, Saskatchewan, June 1983.

Blaireau, A. Letter to the Editor of *The Manitoban*, 5 January 1872, M477f3, Glenbow Archives.

Brasser, T. J. "In Search of Metis Art." National Museum of Man, n. d.

Calihoo, Louie. Letter to Robert Cochrane, 25 February 1939. M. Loggie Papers, D971.23.L832, Glenbow Archives.

Crawford, John. "What Sort of Thing Is Michif?" Work paper for conference, Newberry Library, Chicago, September 1981.

Daniels, H. W., ed. "A Declaration of Metis and Indian Rights," Native Council of Canada, Ottawa, 1979.

Desjarlais, A. Field Report, 12 October 1969. Metis Association of Alberta Files, Glenbow Archives.

Dion, Joseph F. Letter to Jim Brady. Dion Papers, M331, box 2. Glenbow Archives.

Dobbin, M. Interview with H. Pelletier, 17 March 1978, A1324. Saskatchewan Archives Board, Regina.

Foster, John E. "The Country-Born of the Red River Settlements, 1820–1850." Ph.D. diss., University of Alberta, 1973.

Groenland, T. "A Case Study of Scrip Scandal." Research Report on Land Claims, 1978, Metis Association of Alberta, M5848, Glenbow Archives.

Hatt, F. K. "The Response to Directed Social Change on an Alberta Metis Colony." Ph.D. thesis, University of Alberta, 1969.

Ivens, M. Papers. "Ring Hidden in a Tree." Typescript, *Lethbridge Herald*, 20 September 1957, M570.A.I94, Glenbow Archives.

Johnston, Richard. Interview with author. Calgary, Alberta, April 1984.

Lagasse, Jean H. "A Study of the Population of Indian Ancestry Living in Manitoba." Vols. 1–3. Department of Agriculture and Immigration, Winnipeg, 1959

Leduc, Sister. Interview with author. Montreal, Quebec, August 1983.

McKay, Dave. "The Non-People." Indian and Northern Education, University of Saskatchewan, Saskatoon, 1972.

Metis Association of Alberta. "The Metis and the Land in Alberta," Land Claims Research Project 1979–80, M5713, Glenbow Archives.

———. "Origins of the Alberta Metis." Land Claims Research Project 1978–79, M5664, Glenbow Archives.

———. "A Proposal For Progress." Position paper submitted to the Government of the Province of Alberta, 1973.

———. Research Report on Land Claims, 1978, M5848, Glenbow Archives.

Noonan, Edward D., and Percy G. Hodges. "The Saskatchewan Metis," 1943, vol. 7. Metis Historical Collection, Gabriel Dumont Institute, Regina.

Poitras, V. Interview with author. Lebret, Saskatchewan, June 1983.

Rutten, John K. Letter to A. Morris, 30 July 1874. Files, Royal Ontario Museum, Toronto.

Sanders, Douglas. "A Legal Analysis of the Ewing Commission and the Metis Colony System in Alberta." Research Report on Land Claims, 1978, Metis Association of Alberta, M5848, Glenbow Archives.

Sanders, Gilda. Anglican Church Records, 70.387, Provincial Archives of Alberta.

Sharpe, N. "The *Edmonton Bulletin*'s Views on Half-Breed Scrip (1881–1906)." Land Claims Research Final Report, 18 April 1978, pp. 56–73, M5848, Glenbow Archives.

Valentine, V. F. Confidential Report. The Metis of Northern Saskatchewan. Department of Natural Resources, 1955.

Various people. Interviews with author. Saskatoon, November 1982.

NEWSPAPERS

Aboriginal Multi-Media Society of Alberta (Edmonton), vol. 5, 15 April 1983.

Calgary Herald, 15 June 1984.

Edmonton Bulletin, 4 July 1885.

Forgotten People (Ottawa), 8, no. 1 (March 1981).

Metis News (Edmonton), 1, no. 14 (27 November 1972).

New Breed (Regina), August–December 1978; December 1980; July 1982; February–April 1983; December 1983; March 1984, June 1984.

Index

References to captions are in *italic* type.

Aboriginal rights, 15, 20, 38, 40, 41, 76, 97, 105–7, 134, 141, 143–44, 146, 147–49
Alaska Highway, 117
Alberta, 39, 67, 74, 78, 79, 94, 96, 97, 101, 104, 105–7, 130, 133, 134, 141–43
Alberta Native Communications Society, 134
Alberta Tuberculosis Association, 130
Alcoholism, 41, 110, 132. *See also* Whiskey trade
Algonkian, 31
Amisk, Alta., 133
Anglican Church, 21
Annual Conference of Indian and Metis, 134
Association of Metis and Non-Status Indians of Saskatchewan, *143*
Athabasca River, 20, 29, *62, 63*

Bannock, 93, 133
Bannock Town, 124
Basketry, 112–13. *See also* Decorative arts
Batoche, Sask., 43, 45, *45*, 46, 47, 82, 127, *139*
Batoche, Xavier Letendre dit, *45*
Beadwork. *See* Decorative arts
Bear Creek, Sask., 65
Bellegarde, Lena, 96, 111
Bethune, Norman, 15
Bingos, 129
Blackfoot, 67
Black Scots, 11
Block conservation system, 107–10
Boer War, 71
Bois brûlé, 11
Brady, Jim, 96–97, 99, 101, 105, 115–19, 141
Braided rugs, 113. *See also* Decorative arts
Breeds, 11
British Columbia, 144
Buffalo hunt, *11*, 19, 21–26, *23, 25*, 28–29, *29*, 31, 32–35, 36, 39, 40, 41, 56, 57, *57*, 65, 83, 149. *See also* Pemmican
Buffalo Narrows, Sask., 68
Buffalo runners, 23–24, *23*. *See also* Horses

Calder, Jockie, 67
Calgary, Alta., *82*
Calihoo, Felix, *99*
Calihoo, Louie, 65
Calihoo, Victoria, 64
Campbell, Maria, 14, 96, 111, 112
Canada Act, 144
Canadian Expeditionary Force, 82

Canadian Metis Society, 134
Canadian Pacific Railway, 41, 43, 56–57
Capotes, 19, 29, *43*
Card, Dr. B. Y., 130
Card games, 72, 129
Cardinal family, *117*
Card study, 130–32
Carioles, 27, *28*, 67, *53, 70, 89*
Catholic Church, 21, 22, 27, 30, 32, 38, 39, 41–43, 45, *53*, 56, 70, 72, 76, *76*, 78, 97, 101, *104, 127*, 130, *145*
Chalifoux, Isabelle, *30*
Cheadle, Dr. W. B., 12, 27, 30
Cheechum, 111
Churchill, Man., *100*
Churchill River, 92
Class structure, 28–29
Clothing, 10, *11*, 14, 19, *19*, 25, 29–31, *29*, 35, *41, 43*, 46, *66*, 67–70, 79, 84–89, 111, 139–41
Coats, *89*
Colonies, Metis, 101–4, 105, *106*, 130, 133, 141–43, *145*
Comité National des Métis, 36
Confederation, 36
Constitution (of Canada), 10, 143–47, *143*
Constitutional Conferences, 146
Cosley, Joseph, 83
Country-born, 11
Coyotes, 96
Cree, 12, *84*, 105
Crown lands, 93
Cumberland House, Sask., 119
Cupar, Sask., 96
Cuthand, Rev. Adam, 134

Dances, 26–27, *26, 71*, 111, 129–30
Daniels, Stan, 15, 133
Dechene, J. M., 97–99, *99*
Declaration of Metis Rights, 15
Decorative arts, 14, 22, 24, 27, 29, 30–31, 48–53, 70–72, 84–89, 113–15, *129*, 141. *See also* Basketry; Braided rugs; Clothing; L'Assomption sashes
Department of Indian Affairs, 82
Department of Municipal Affairs, 143
Department of Natural Resources, 119
Department of Social Services, 143
Department of the Interior, 76
Depression, 94, 96, 111, 115
Desjarlais, Harold, 134
Diefenbaker, John, *131*
Dion, Joe, 93–95, 96–97, 101, 105
Dobbin, Murray, 135

Dogsleds, 27, *28*, 67, *70, 89, 145*
Dominion Lands Act, 43
Donaldson, Mary Jean, 96
Duck Lake, Sask., 46, *104*
Dumas, Michel, 44
Dumont, Gabriel, 43, 44, *44*, 45, 46, 47, 56, 97

Edmonton, Alta., *70*
Edmonton Bulletin, 75, 76
Education, 19, 31, 38, 43, 64, 72, 76, 78, 79, 93–94, 97, 101, *104*, 105, 107, 113–15, 119, 124, *127*, 133, 138, 141, 143, 144. *See also* Mission schools
Embroidery. *See* Decorative arts
English, 11, 12. *See also* European heritage
English Canadians, 15, 56
English Half-breeds, 12, 20, 21, 36, 39, 44, 47. *See also* Scottish Half-breeds
European contact, 10
European heritage, 11, 12, 15, 18, 19, 21, 22, *25*, 26, 29, 30, 41–43, *43*, 72, 73, *79*, 84, *89*, 111, 117–19, 130, 138, 139, 149
Ewers, J., 31
Ewing, A. F., 99
Ewing Commission, 97–101, 104

Falcon, Pierre, 111
Falher, Rev. Father, *99*
Family bonds, 10, 19, 96, 119, *128*, 129, 130, 132, 139
Farming, 12, 20, 21, 28, 36, 39, 43, 64, 65, 72, 76, 77, 78, 101–4, 107–10, *113*, 119, 124, 133
Federation of Metis Settlements, 141–43
Fiddles, 27, *53*, 111, 129, 130, 138, *149*
Firebags, *53*
Firefighters, *146*
First Ministers' Conferences, 144, 149
First World War, 79–83, *80, 82, 83*, 92, 115
Firth, Mr., *71*
Fish Creek, Sask., 46
Fishing, 19, 20, 65, 94, 104, 117, 133
Fishing Lake, Alta., 93, 94
Fishing Lake, Sask., *110*
Forcier, Jean Baptiste, 75
Fort Carlton, 30
  Chipewyan, 93, *104*
  Garry, 31, 36, 38
  McKay, 67
  Qu'Appelle, 96, 111
  Rae, 93
  Resolution, 93
  St. John, *57*

Smith, 93
Tuyau, 124
Vermilion, 134
France, 117
Freighters, *19*, 35–36, 39, *62*, 64, *64*, 65
Freight trains. *See* Red River carts
French, 11, 12, 26, 27, 117–19, 130. *See also* European heritage
French Canadians, 15, 18–19, 56, 78, 117
French Half-breeds. *See* French Metis
French Metis, 12, 18–19, 20, 21–22, 36, 39, *41*, 44, 46, 47, 56, *57*, 61, 75, 117
Frog Lake Reserve, 93–95
Fur Marketing Board, 107
Furniture, 14, 28, 64, 110, 111–12, 127, 133
Fur trade, 10–11, 12, *13*, 14, 18–19, 20, 21, 32, 35, 36, 41, 56, *89*, 107, 110, 132

Gabriel's Crossing, 43, *44*
Gambling, 24, 27, 72, 75, 129
Giroux, Leonidas, *99*
Gladstone, Alex, *81*
Gladstone, Mrs. Robert, *79*
Gophers, 96
Grande Prairie, Alta., 65
Grant, Cuthbert, 20
Great Lakes, 20
Green Lake, Sask., 110, *127*, 129, *129*
Grey Nuns (Grey Sisters of Charity), 21, 78, 113
Grouard, Alta., 65, 97
Guns, 23, 24, 29, 32, *53*, 65, 66, 67

Halfbreed. *See* Campbell, Maria
Half-breed, term, 11–12. *See also* English Half-breeds; French Metis; Metis; Scottish Half-breeds
Half-Breed Commission. *See* Ewing Commission
Half Breeds Running Buffalo, 23
Halfcast and His Two Wives, A, *11*
Handkerchief, 30, 67–68
Headgear, 29–30, *89*, 139
Heron, Francis, *30*
High Prairie, Alta., 131
Hiverants, 31–32, 39, *69*
Hope, Adrian, 134
Horses, 23–24, *23*, 27, 28, *57*, 65, *71*, 75, *122*
Household items, *53*
House of Commons, 39
Housing, 28, 31–32, *32*, 61, 64, 68, *69*, 107–10, 111–12, 124–27, 131, 133, 134, 144
Hudson Bay, 11
Hudson's Bay Company, 18, 26, *30*, 32, 36, 40, *61*, 65, 67, 68, 107
Hunting, 12, 18, 20, *23*, *57*, *58*, 65, 76, 83, 92, 94, 96, 104, 107, 109, 114, 119, 132

Indian Act, 94–95

Indian Metis Friendship Centre, 134
Interlakes Fish Pool, 104–5
Irish, 12
Isbister, James, 44
Islay, Alta., *117*

Jackets, buckskin, 10, *89*, 139
Jasper, Alta., *79*
Jiarobia, 67
Julien, Henri, *32*

Kane, Paul, *23*, 27, *89*
Keg River, *113*, *115*
Klondike Gold Rush, 65, 117
Knife, 66–67
Korean War, 122, *123*

Labourers, 61, *61*, 64, 65, 92, 96, 124, 132, *146*, *147*
Lac la Biche, *71*
Lac Ste. Anne, 64, *145*
Lacombe, Father Albert, *76*, 78
Lagasse, Jean, 122, 123, 124, 127
Lagasse study, 122–24, 127
Land allotments, 40–41, 44
Land claims. *See* Aboriginal rights
Land scrip. *See* Scrip
Language, 12, 14, 36, 38, 43, 75, 105, 123, 132, 143, 144
L'Association des Métis d'Alberta et les Territoires au Nord-Ouest, 97, 99, *99*, 101, 105, 117. *See also* Metis Association of Alberta
L'Assomption sashes, 19, 29, 31, *43*, *89*, 139. *See also* Decorative arts
Lebret, Sask., *123*, 129–30
Leduc, Sister, 113–15
Leggings, 29, 111
Lepine, Ambroise, *39*
Lepine family, *41*
Lesser Slave Lake, 65, *74*, 93
Lestock, Sask., 110
Little Black Devils, 82
Lougheed, Peter, 15, *41*
L'Union Nationale Métisse St. Joseph, 123

McCallum, Harriet, 92–93
Macdonald, Sir John A., 36, 39, 56–57, 73
McDonald brothers, *70*
McDougall, Lieut. Gov. William, 36
McKay, "Young," *24*
Mackenzie River area, 64
Manitoba, 39, 40, 64, 92, 107, 122–23, 124, 134
Manitoba Act, 38, 40–41
Manitoba Metis Federation, 134, 144
Maple Creek, Sask., *43*
Meighen, Arthur, 93
Methodist Church, 21
Metis, definition of, 11, 14–15, 99, 123–24, 134, 139, 146–47; origin of term, 11–12; relations with Indians, 14, 31, 61, 70, 72, 73, 75, 77, 79, 107, 124, 131, 132, 134, 135, 138, 143; sign language for, 22; stereotypes, 12, 27, *41*, 57, 101, 133, 139
Métis anglaise, 11
Metis Association of Alberta, 133–34, 144. *See also* L'Association Métis d'Alberta
Metis Association of Saskatchewan, 132–33, 144
Metis associations, 15, 143, 144–46
Metis Betterment Act, 104, 141
Metis Development Branch, 143
Metis Heritage Days, *139*
Metis National Council, 14, 144, 146
Michif, 12
Middleton, Maj. Gen. Frederick, 45, 46, 47
Miller, Dorothy, 133
Milton and Cheadle, 12. *See also* Cheadle, W. B.
Missionaries, 20–21. *See also* Religion
Mission schools, 30, 31, 70, 72, 76, 113–15
Moberley family, *79*
Moccasins, 10, 26, 29, 30, 31, 35, 70, 111, *129*
Montana, 39, 44, 45, 64
Montreal, 18, 20
Morris, Alexander, 72

National Indian Brotherhood, 134
Native Council of Canada, 134, 143, 144–46
Native heritage, 10, 12, 14, 15, 18, 19, 20, 26, 29, 30, 31, 41, *43*, 72, 75, 79, 83, 84, *89*, 105, 113, 124, 134, 135, 138, *139*, *143*, 149
Native religion, 21, 72
Nault, André, 36, *39*
Nault, Dan, *81*
Needlework. *See* Decorative arts
New nation, 14, 149
New Year celebrations, 130
Nonstatus Indians, 14, 105, 124, 134, 143
Nontreaty Indians. *See* Nonstatus Indians
Noonan and Hodges, 105–7
Norquay, John, 39
Norris, Malcolm, 96–97, 99, *99*, 101, 104–5, 115, 132, 133, 141
North Battleford, Sask., *145*
North-West, 18, 36
North West Company, 18, 19, 20
North-West Half-Breed Commissions, 73, 74
North-West Mounted Police, 46, *46*, 65. *See also* Royal Canadian Mounted Police.
North-West Rebellion (1885), 37, 45–47, *45*, 47, 56–57, 65, 67, 72, 97
Northwest Territories, 39, 41–44, 45, 46–47, 57, 66, 72, 73, 78
Norway House, 21, 26
Nor'West, Henry, *83*

Oblates (of Mary Immaculate), 21, 32, 78
Ojibwa, 11, 12
Oman, *100*
Ontario, 43

159

Orangemen, 38–39, 56
Order of the Sash, 89
Orkney Islands, 19
Ouellette, Moise, 44

Parliament, 36, 38, *38*, 39, 93
Patois, 12
Peace River area, 64
Pelletier, Henry, 110
Pembina, Minn., 21, *26*
Pemmican, 19, 20, 21, 24–26, 35, 39, 92, 110
Pilgrimages, *104, 145*
Pincher Creek, Alta., *81*
Pipes, 19, *19*, 23, 27, *53*, 66, 67
Pipes (unit of measurement), 19
Plains Indians, 22
Poitras, Adolphus, *80*
Poitras, E. J., *118*
Poitras, J. G., *118*
Poitras, Pierre, 96
Poitras, St. Pierre, *80*
Poitras, St. Paul, *80*, 117
Poitras, Victor, *123*
Population estimates, 15, 36, 123
Portages, 19, *64*, 92–93
Presbyterian Church, 21
Prince Albert, Sask., 43, 46, 96
Protestant Church, 21, 27, 36. *See also* Orangemen
Provisional government (Batoche), 45
Provisional government (Red River), 36, 38, *38*

Qu'Appelle Valley, Sask., 65
Quebec, 21, 22, 29, 44–45, *89*, 117
Quillwork. *See* Decorative arts

Racial prejudice, 12, 27, 39, *41*, 57, 59, 61–64, 72, 73, 77, 110, 119, 123, 124, 132, 133
Ralph, Julian, 57–59
Rebellion. *See* North-West Rebellion; Red River Insurrection
Red Deer, Alta., *83*
Red River, 20, 26, 36
Red River carts, *13, 19*, 22, *24, 25*, 32–35, *61*
Red River (colony), 14, 20–21, 27, 28–29, 30, 31, 32, 35, 36–39, *38*, 40, *40*, 43, 44, *45*, 57–59, 61, 64
Red River Insurrection (1869–70), 36–38, *36, 39*, 44, 45, 47
Red River jig, 26, 129, 130, 138
Regina, Sask., 47, *143*
Relief, 65, 95, 97, 105, 110, 123. *See also* Welfare
Religion. *See* Grey Nuns; Missionaries; Mission schools; Native religion; Oblates; Orangemen; sects under various names
Religious pictures, 28, *53*, 127
Riel, Louis, 10, 36, 38–39, *38, 39*, 43, 44–45, *45*, 46–47, *47*, 56–57, 72, 82, 97, 149
Riel, Louis (Sr.), 32, 36
Riel, Patrick (Paddy), 82
Rindisbacher, Peter, *11*
Road allowances, 64
Rockies, 64, *95*
Rogers, W. A., *24*
Rooster Town, 124
Ross, Alexander, 27–28, 30, 39
Ross, Joseph, 105
Royal Canadian Mounted Police, 96, 119. *See also* North-West Mounted Police
Rupert's Land, *13*

Saddle Lake Reserve, Alta., 78
Saddles, *23, 53*
St. Albert, Alta., 47, 65, 75
St. Jean Baptiste Day, 72
St. Laurent, Man., *45*
St. Lawrence River, 11
St. Paul, Alta., *80*, 117
St. Paul, Minn., *28*, 32, 35
St. Paul des Métis, Alta., 78
St. Peter's Mission, Mon., 45
Sash. *See* L'Assomption sash
Saskatchewan, 31, 39, 61, 74, 78, 92, 105, 107–10, 117, 132, 134
Saskatchewan Herald, 44
Saskatchewan Metis Society, 105–7, *131*
Saskatchewan River, 19, 127
Sayer, Guillaume, 32
Scandinavian, 12
Scotland, 19, 22
Scots, 11, 12, 19, 21, 26, 27, 130. *See also* European heritage
Scott, Thomas, 38–39
Scottish Half-breeds, 21, 39, 44, 67. *See also* English Half-breeds
Scrip, 73–74, *73*, 75, 76–77, 78, 79, 93, 99, 107, 147. *See also* Scrip and Treaty Commission; Scrip Commission; Scrip commissions; Scrip speculation; Street Commission
Scrip and Treaty Commission, 74, *74*
Scrip Commission, 74
Scrip commissions, 74–76, 77
Scrip speculation, 76, 93, 147
Second World War, 115–19, *117, 118, 123*
Secord, Richard, 93
Selkirk, Lord, 20
Semple, Governor, 20
Seneca root, 65, 92, 124
Seton, Ernest Thompson, 67–70
Settlements. *See* Colonies, Metis
Seven Oaks, Battle of, 20, 111
Shaganappi, 22
Shawls, 30, *66*
Sinclair, Jim, 143
Sioux, 84
Skirts, 30, 111

Sleighs, *71, 122*
Smokey Hollow, 124
Snowshoes, 10, 32, 68
Social and Economic Research Office, 122
Southesk, Earl of, 29–30, 31
South Saskatchewan Regiment, *118*
South Saskatchewan River, 59
Street Commission, 73–74
Sturgeon, 93
Surveys, 36, 43, *115*
Sutherland family, *40*

Talent contests, 130
Talopime, 93
Tea, 27, 93, 110, 133
Teadance, *139*
Thatcher, Ross, 132
Therien, Father, 78
Thomas, Mary, *41*
Tomkins, Pete, 96–97, *99*
Tourism, 132
Traders, free, 32, 35–36, *35*, 65
Trapping, 12, 14, 18, 19, 20, 39, 65, 76, 92–93, 94, *94, 95*, 96, 97, 104, 107–10, 112, 119, *124*, 132, 143
Treaty Indians, 41, 76, 79, 82
Treaty rights, 15, 72, 73, 75, 76, 78, 79, 82, 94–95, 124, 143, 144, 146
Trottier, Brian, 15
Trottier, Corbett, 94–95
Trottier family, *110*
Trudeau, Pierre E., 138, *143*
Trunks, 32, *89*
Tuberculosis, 64, 101, 130–31, 133
Tuppies, 67
Turtle Mountain, S. D., 12
Tytler, P. F., 29

United States, 39, 40, 64
Upper Canada, 36

Van Horne, W. C., 57
Voyageurs, 12, 18–19, 29, 111

Wabamun, Alta., 104
Waistcoat, *89*
Wall pocket, *53*
Webster, Mrs. Gerald, *116*
Welfare, 96, 97, 110, 119, 123, 132. *See also* Relief
Welfare Council of Greater Winnipeg, 132, 134
West, Rev. J., 21
Whips, 67
Whiskey trade, 41, 64. *See also* Alcoholism
Wild rice, 124, *147*
Winnipeg, Lake, 19
Wissakodewinmi, 11
Wood, Eliza, 82
Wood Mountain, Sask., *32*

York boats, 19, *62, 63*

Louis Riel in 1884. Photograph by C. A. Zimmerman, courtesy Glenbow Museum, NA 2631-2

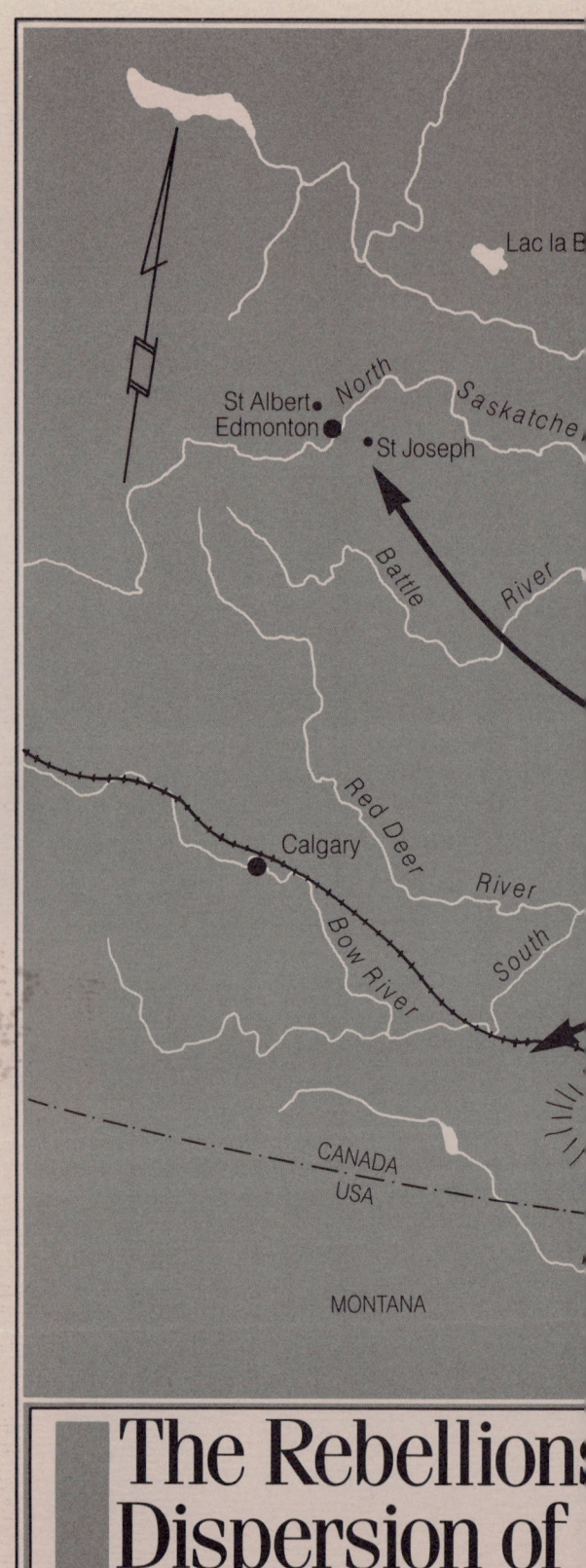

The Rebellions
Dispersion of

++++++++++++ CANADIAN PACIFIC
⬅ METIS DISPERSION

0   100   200
0   200

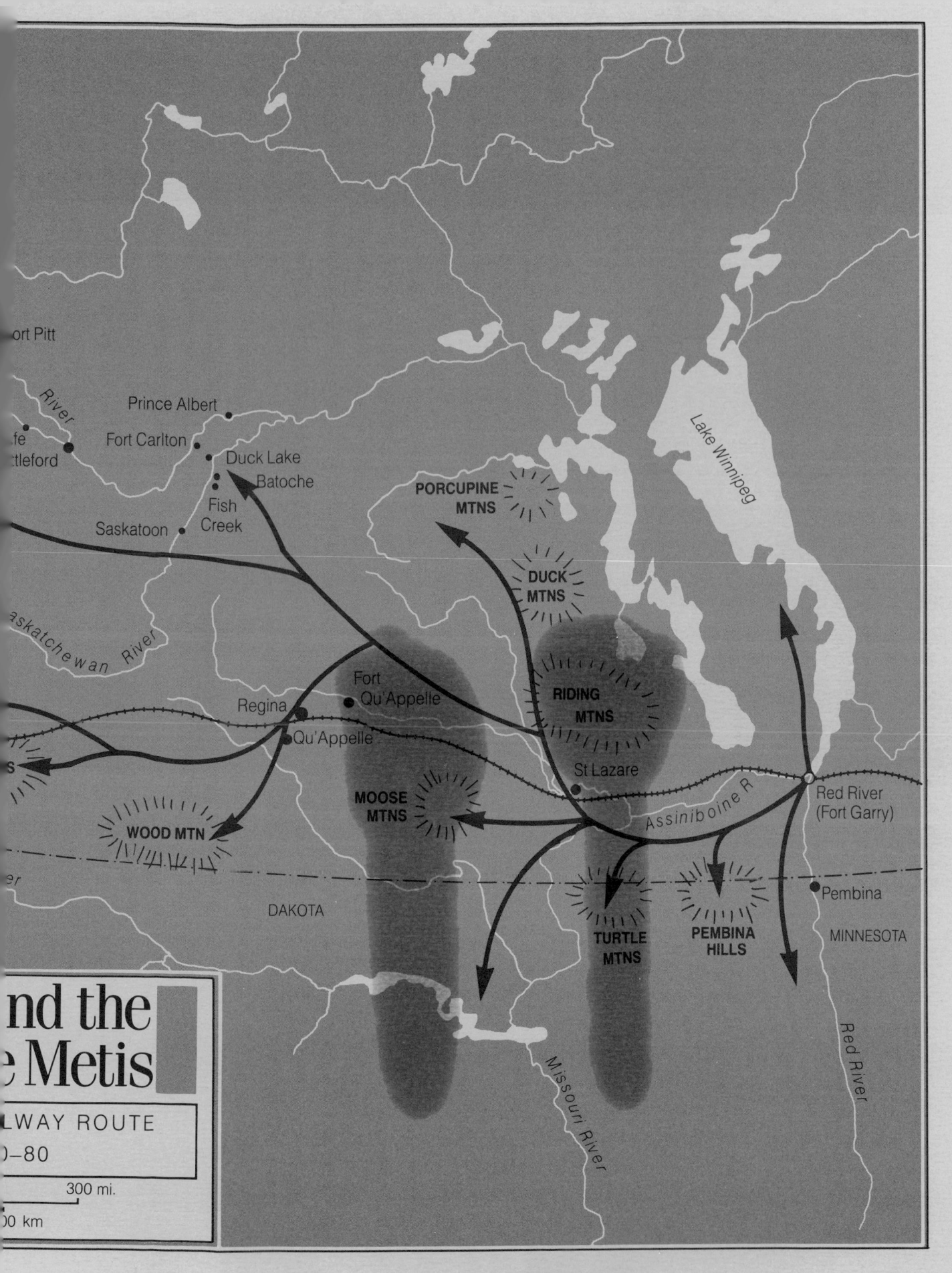

Date Due

APR 19 1995		
APR 07 1997		
APR 20 1997		
OCT 23 2000		

```
971.    Harrison, Julia D.
00497   Metis
HAR
1985
                    4815
```

```
971.    Harrison, Julia D.
00497   Metis
HAR
1985
                    4815
```

ALBERTA COLLEGE LIBRARY
10050 MACDONALD DRIVE
EDMONTON, AB   T5J 2B7